2-13-68

MISSION TO PERU

MISSION to PERU

A Story of Papal Volunteers

DAN B. McCARTHY

THE BRUCE PUBLISHING COMPANY / MILWAUKEE

Library of Congress Catalog Card Number: 67-28889

© 1967 The Bruce Publishing Company
Made in the United States of America

1441820

To Rosa
who turned our thoughts South

ACKNOWLEDGMENT

Heartfelt appreciation is expressed here to those who contributed in any way to our work in Peru, or who have promoted — and continue to support — the cause of the Papal Volunteers for Latin America.

Our gratitude, too, to editors and friends who have granted us permission to use quotes within these pages. Their cooperation was splendid and their information invaluable. Thank you for helping.

PREFACE

"If a free society cannot help the many who
are poor, it cannot save the few who are rich."
— John F. Kennedy

Christ is in agony in Latin America. Thousands upon thousands
of good people there will not see a doctor in their lifetime, they
will go to sleep hungry day after day, they will see a priest as
Catholics in Latin lands only occasionally, if at all between birth
and death.

How can we without pain hear their call and lightly dismiss it?
How can we, blessed by God's abundance in the United States, help
them not? How can we ignore the pitiful clamoring of so many
neglected people suffering material and spiritual want in Latin
America?

Why is it that we, not lacking food, shelter, health, clothing, education, employment, and spiritual direction, remain aware of their
misery only from a distance?

We were but two who went to Latin America, counted among
the growing numbers of North American Catholic laymen of service
to the Church there. This narrative unfolded here is in no wise the
official story of the Papal Volunteers for Latin America. It is a personal account of three years in the missions, reviewing our work
and associations with Peruvians, U. S. religious, and missionaries from
other lands assigned there. Included are moments spent with Peruvian, Vatican City, and U. S. hierarchy of the Church. We met tour-

ix

ing fellow citizens there, too, and many others on U. S. government and private industry payrolls. We visited and sometimes worked with U. S. missioners of Protestant sects. Perhaps by actions we demonstrated why my wife Mary Ellen and I were in Peru as Papal Volunteers for Latin America.

"We must give some time to our fellowman," said Dr. Albert Schweitzer.

"The only way the people of Burma will ever believe that I meant what I've done for them is for me to die here among them," said Dr. Gordon Seagrave.

"The suffering people of Southeast Asia, the 'have-nots' of the world, needed help. Somehow I must find a way to bring it to them," said Dr. Tom Dooley.

How will the next great man say it? For there will be another one, and another one, and another one . . . but one man cannot do it alone. More of us must help!

—Dan B. McCarthy

CONTENTS

CHAPTER I

GOING LATIN VIA BUS

"No one today in a world where distance no longer counts can give the excuse that the needs of his faraway brother are not known to him, nor can one say that the task of helping his brother is not his concern."

— Pope John XXIII

Three short hours had passed since we crossed the International Bridge spanning the Rio Grande, answered the questions in our limited Spanish of the Mexican customs inspectors, then roared onward toward three years of voluntary mission work with the Catholic Church in Latin America.

There would be no turning back now, and as each Pan American highway kilometer was chalked up, taking us farther away from our homes, families, friends, and security, each one of us volunteer missioners would have admitted some such fleeting thoughts as:

"Am I finally on the way?"

"Do I have what is asked of a lay missioner?"

"Will I be able to take it?"

Our passports had been stamped "official visa" by the Peruvian consulate in Washington, D. C., with a note on one of the pages that we were on an apostolic mission as *Voluntarios del Papa*. On our arrival in the land of the Incas, we would be known as Volunteers of the Pope, come to help shore up social justice, improve standards of living, and assist in strengthening the place of Peruvians in the Mystical Body of Christ. "Help others to help others to help themselves" was our watchword.

The Chicago national headquarters of the Papal Volunteers for Latin America officially listed us as its second pioneering lay group assigned below the border in late 1961, about a year after the beloved Pope John initiated the somewhat visionary program. Our group in the coming years was to be identified by the initials PAVLA.

The bus was jam-packed as only a Latin American public bus can be. Most of the passengers were Mexican and most of them were asleep. Some of the dozen North Americans on board still searched for sleep the way one does on an overland bus journey of many miles. Only the whine of heavy-duty tires on Highway 85, stretching south of Nuevo Laredo to Monterrey, and occasional chuffs and complaining snorts of the motor were heard as the driver shifted gears. Blasts of the air horn at irregular intervals sent people and their laden burros or oxcarts scurrying to the side of the road. "How do they keep from being struck down on these dark roads?" I wondered, craning my neck forward at each blast of the horn, because the bus rarely slackened speed. Soon the bus began to labor as it began the winding ascent into the Sierra Madre mountains.

A small circle of steam appeared momentarily with each breath against my windowpane, as I peered at the darkness, seeing nothing really, taking in new thoughts, letting out a deep breath now and then, sort of unwinding after the days of tense, emotional farewells with family and friends back home.

The weather had turned cold incredibly fast after sunset as the bus left the cactus-covered desert floor and climbed to the higher altitudes of the foothills. It was late January, but what a difference from the Kansas weather! When we entered Mexican territory, we shed our coats under the warm sun of a winter afternoon. The day before we had slid and shivered through heavy snow en route to the Wichita bus terminal.

In the afternoon the warm weather and the unwinding of red tape with the Mexican customs people had made us thirsty; consequently, one of the priests in our group and I went out of the stuffy bus and customs terminal and walked a half block along a sun-soaked, dusty street of veranda-shaded store fronts and stepped inside the open door of a Nuevo Laredo cantina at the corner for a glass of cool beer. Back at the terminal border inspectors were demanding another look at our baggage claim tickets — all of which were in my pocket!

"Baggage teekits!" said the Mexican official very officially. "Baggage tickets!" repeated members of our group. "Quick! Where's Dan?" One person had been given all the bus tickets to care for; another, the official papers; and I, the baggage claim checks. The priest in charge felt that when it came time to see, stamp, punch, or do whatever had to be done to our tickets, papers, and the like, it would be better to have one person responsible for the group.

A youth worker, Wayne Paxton, who had been a lifeguard at Kansas swimming pools and taught Cuban refugee children in Wichita, hurried in search of us. Earlier he had heard us discuss a cooling libation. Using bits of Spanish with a policeman on the corner and making the motions of a person lifting a glass to his mouth, he finally got his question across. The policeman pointed to the cantina, where a canvas awning rolled down in front shaded the cafe from the rays of the setting sun.

Paxton swooped inside and halted abruptly when he saw us right next to the open door. Before we could remark, jokingly, how thirsty he must be coming in that fast, he shouted, "Baggage tickets, hurry!"

He grabbed the tickets and sprinted off.

According to our watches the bus was due to leave in 15 minutes U. S. time. But the bus actually departed on mañana time, 45 minutes later, and it wasn't our baggage tickets that held up the departure. This was our first experience with time and timetables below the border.

On the Pan American highway between Nuevo Laredo and Monterrey there were two more federal inspection checkpoints. Here there was no additional rummaging through suitcases or duffle bags. The inspectors simply saw that the seals attached at the border had been untouched, looked carefully at our passports and Mexican tourist permits, and departed. The bus lurched forward in a chatter of shifting gears.

Contemplating the newness of our assignment, I turned to my wife, Mary Ellen, who was stirring now in the seat beside me, dreaming perhaps of what nursing the sick would be like in a Peruvian mission post. I whispered: "So this is why some of the folks back home flipped when we said we were going to Peru."

"It's not like Kansas City so far," she replied drowsily, at the moment more interested in sleep than in conversation. Unable to snatch sleep in short takes and groggy after having passed the previous night in another bus above the Rio Grande, I resumed my gazing into the black night, trying again to imagine what the Mexican landscape was like while memories of those final days of preparation in Kansas came to mind.

The last days before departure had not been easy.

Pulling up stakes in the suburbs for a three-year assignment in Latin America on the volunteer's dollar-a-day stipend for personal needs is not normal in the light of today's swinging sense of normality. (Room and board are covered by the parish or organization for whom you work in Latin America.) Burgeoning suburbia, of course, makes almost mandatory the status symbols of backyard patios, boat and motor, second car, charge accounts, and outdoor fireplace. In such surroundings we had managed without the second car or boat and without giving in to the temptation to open charge accounts.

The day the "For Sale" sign appeared on our front lawn we spilled out our secret to inquiring neighbors. Yes, we told them, we've made definite plans and are cutting back on material possessions. For a half year we've been getting ready. We've shifted our emphasis to a new value, an apostolic value, which we pray will ready us for our mission work in Peru. We feel we have what Reverend Vincent Giese called the "apostolic itch."

"Going where?" the neighbor across the street shrieked. "Peru?" He said later that he was hoping we had said Peoria or some other place not so far out.

"To do lay missionary work for the Catholic church!" his wife exclaimed.

When she regained her composure, she said, "Oh, Mary Ellen,

you won't be able to go to the beauty shop with us on Fridays any more!"

Most of our neighbors and relatives reacted to our disclosure with outbursts of disbelief.

During the six months before departure we had asked each other repeatedly: "Can we really leave relatives and friends, home and furniture, TV, bowling league and beauty shop, paydays and income tax?" Some of these things we'd never miss; others, we'd give up reluctantly, we admitted.

"Kooky" as the idea seemed to everyone, we felt that we could trust our own intent and apostolic aims. One of the most definite steps toward committing ourselves was the discontinuing of our foster children care. Having no children of our own, we had for several years given care and love to pre-school children, in our home, for the Catholic Charities of the Archdiocese of Kansas City in Kansas.

Rosa, the last of our foster children, came to us when she was only 10 days old. She was of Mexican parentage. We loved her every minute, as did some of the neighbors, who brought over little things for her.

Rosa was with us for about four months, long enough for her to fatten up, start smiling toothlessly, and make various little noises.

After she left us and was adopted by a Mexican couple, Papal Volunteer work became part of our almost daily conversation. Mary Ellen and I recalled the days Rosa was with us and we could not help wondering if Our Lady of Guadalupe helped put Rosa into our home in order to spark an awareness in us of thousands of neglected Rosas and Pedros in Latin America, and to dilute our material thinking with deeper spiritual values and later send us to work among the Latins.

After the final inspection stop, the bus was again humming along the highway with most of our PAVLA group settled down quietly, trying for a nap before arrival in Monterrey. Earlier, we had recited the rosary aloud and had sung several hymns. I wondered what the Mexican passengers who were unable to understand English supposed we Yankees were up to.

I felt then and still feel that the close confinement of a public bus is not a propitious place to parade our faith before other passengers without giving them the option of expressing a preference. Yet, I joined our group in reciting the rosary aloud and my voice, not good for singing, creaked along during the hymns. My contribution, I know, caused the passenger seated ahead of us to take the pillow from behind his head and jam it against his left ear, while pressing his right ear against the white doily fastened to the back rest.

The first group of Papal Volunteers had traveled overland from Kansas City to Mexico City six months before us. They prayed aloud and sang hymns, too, but in a chartered bus, private and exclusive for PAVLA volunteers, their families, and friends. We had not yet heard the stirring voices of ecumenism. The first session of Vatican Council II was months away and front-page pictures of nuns out in the streets, holding hands with Christians of all races and creeds, were not so commonplace as they are now.

After the comfortable private cars (which we sold before leaving home) or speedy jet travel, the idea of journeying some 1,750 miles in a bus between Kansas City and Mexico City seemed a bit radical.

"What! You're going to Mexico City by bus?" That question was shouted across a room at one of the bon voyage gatherings as if we were going to try crossing the Pacific Ocean on a balsa raft or bicycle to Cape Horn.

Trying to be casual or blasé, we replied: "Oh, certainly! You see so much more that way than when you fly. And think how educational and profitable it'll be to start rubbing elbows with the Latins from the very moment we're over the border."

We avoided mentioning the basic reason, of course. In those beginning days the practice of mission frugality was very, very new to us. It was not easy to say, "And we'll be able to travel so much cheaper."

As the lights brightened inside, Mary Ellen stirred. Shortly thereafter the bus stopped at the roadside in the little town of Cienaga de Flores, just north of the Salinas river about 25 miles from Monterrey, to exchange several passengers carrying sacks and panchos.

My shoes were off and a gaudy pair of heavy red sox, good for snowy Kansas weather, showed prominently in the lighted bus, especially the one on my right foot propped on my left knee. My wife, awake now, wondered why those sox hadn't gone with the St. Vincent de Paul clothing. "Such loud things," she sighed. Before leaving, we had successfully whittled our personal luggage to 60 pounds to meet the maximum allowance of the Peruvian airlines that would fly us out of Mexico to Peru. But the red sox somehow stayed with us. Looking at them now, I felt they would not be unappreciated in Mexico, especially after having already seen many people without even shoes.

The lights in the bus dimmed again. The few bright lights of the little town called "marsh of flowers" faded away. New anxiety stirred within me as I realized that gone for the years ahead were the comforting islands of security which U. S. cities just naturally afforded native travelers. Below the border, each town, city, or nation would be completely strange. Another people's culture, customs, values, and daily life must become ours. We must become a very part of these cultures and customs. We were not coming among the Latins as tourists, arriving, looking, exclaiming, and leaving.

As the Papal Nuncio to Peru, Archbishop Romolo Carboni, was to tell us later: "We must bring the very best from our culture to these Latin lands, exchanging it for their very best. We will give and receive in the mission apostolate."

Seeing cultural differences as each mile passed, we realized that our lives, lived so far in a matter-of-fact manner in our own land, would now, of necessity, be lived amid the tremendous struggle of neglected people. There would be new demands on us for perseverance and a vital need for spiritual guidance and direction.

Most of us were to complete our three-year assignments; a few would not. For Mary Ellen and me there was a willing, helping hand in our initial adjustment waiting in the person of Dr. Rafael Hinjosa, who had promised to meet us at the bus terminal in Monterrey, his home town. During Mary Ellen's nursing days at St. Mary's hospital in Kansas City, Mo., we became close friends of Dr. Hinjosa. While interning at the hospital, he visited our home in Overland Park upon occasion, sometimes bringing along several other Mexican doctors for a Saturday afternoon of badminton and a cookout with the food spiced to suit Mexican taste. Dr. Hinjosa had written and invited us to visit him and his family in Monterrey.

As our bus wheeled into the Monterrey depot shortly before midnight, completing the first leg of the travels from Nuevo Laredo, the Papal Volunteers and two priests said to us: "Remember, instead of U. S. handshakes, let's see the big abrazo!" (The bear hug greeting with appropriate thumpings on the back.)

Before the bus came to a stop, we saw Dr. Hinjosa from the window, his coat collar turned up against the brisk night air. Halfway to the terminal entrance the young doctor met us. Mary Ellen was the first to greet him with the abrazo. Then she stepped back to make way for me and there on Mexican soil, outside a crowded bus terminal, I engaged in my first abrazo, feeling not quite so self-conscious as I had expected.

From behind I heard Yankee cheers, but I didn't turn around. As Sister Thomas More, a Kansas college instructor, had told us at one of the PAVLA orientation sessions, this seemingly insignificant act was our beginning "of the wedding of the cultures." And we were on our honeymoon.

Our two priests, Father Michael Lies, former PAVLA assistant national director in Chicago and now a pastor in the Diocese of Wichita, and Father John Stitz, from the Archdiocese of Kansas City in Kansas, stepped from the bus during the brief stopover to meet Dr. Hinjosa and his mother, Mrs. Juan Hinjosa, and followed suit with abrazos. The priests reboarded the departing bus and we remained behind to stay over Tuesday night and to take the bus Wednesday noon for Mexico City, a twelve-hour ride from Monterrey.

No other gringos were in sight. With Dr. Hinjosa at the wheel of his car we felt that our life in Latin America was now truly beginning. Kansas, hamburgers, the Starlight Theatre, occasional Saturday night TV, the old neighborhood, the familiar work desk, the basketball backboards pulled back in the school gym during Sunday Mass . . . all of these were becoming distant things to us.

Self-consciously we tossed out a Spanish word or phrase as we gave the language a try and the Hinjosas sensed this. Dr. Rafael had explained to them that we would begin our language course of four months upon arrival in Lima. For the moment his gringo friends would be relying upon some hurried Spanish sessions taken during preparation days.

The PAVLA program calls for four months' training on Latin American soil. During our time — in the early days of the program — only the schools in Cuernavaca, Mexico, where Spanish language, Latin culture and history are taught, and in Belem and Petropolis, Brazil, for Portuguese, were functioning. Today there are training schools in Washington, D. C., Mexico City, Puerto Rico, and in some U. S. dioceses.

We arrived at the Hinjosa home along a quiet, narrow street just past midnight. Mary Ellen, after repeating "Hace frio" (it's cold) so many times to Dr. Hinjosa's mother, father, sister, brother, and sister-in-law, finally and desperately turned to the doctor and asked him to be her interpreter so she could get some other thoughts across. I had asked the same favor of him.

During the next 12 hours in the home of this kind Mexican family we had our first glimpse of Latin home life. Here we learned why the young doctor, soon to be married, spoke so proudly of his new, 100-gallon electric hot water heater that stood crated in a corner of his bedroom, awaiting the day he and his new bride would have it installed in their own home.

A U. S. couple, moving into rental housing, takes for granted an unlimited supply of hot water. Taken for granted, also, would be light fixtures in the walls and ceilings, mirror-covered medicine chests, and, of course, toilet seats in the bathroom. Below the border the incoming tenants bring these fixtures with them.

After Mass the next morning, despite our telling our hostess that, as light eaters, we'd only want toast and coffee, the breakfast included eggs, T-bone steaks, potatoes, and beans, all topped off with fruit. The sincerity of the Hinjosas hospitality was demonstrated splendidly in this breakfast.

On a window in the front door of the Hinjosa home was a sticker on which was a line drawing of a fish, and above it the message: "El

Simbolo del Cristianismo destuirā al Comunismo" (The Christian symbol will destroy communism). Many Monterrey people were placing such notices in their homes, the Hinjosas said, as the movement to embrace Christianity was taking deeper root.

In the shadow of Monterrey's Saddle Mountain, which rises 5,703 feet above the city in grand majesty, abrazos all around took place that noon we departed. We were to use the Latin sign of endearment often in the years ahead on the slopes of the Andes Mountains, in streets of Lima, the altiplano of the high sierra, the jungles of northeast Peru and Brazil, and in the foothills and towering capital of La Paz in Bolivia.

Warmed by the hospitality of the Hinjosas, we began the 600-mile bus ride over the Pan American highway to Mexico City in higher spirits than at any time since our decision to leave our home in the United States. Our spirits were buoyed by the anticipation of working with people of the same race as the charming Hinjosas.

Too many centuries the Latin *peon* or *campesino* has been relegated to below-average citizenship in his respective nation. He has almost constantly suffered physical hunger, illiteracy, spiritual denial at the hands of an elite, profit-hungry oligarchy. Priest-poor parishes of his Catholic homeland have been unable to give him his religious due. The aim of our apostolic assignments in Peru was to help give the Latins a better chance. Our efforts, we were cautioned, might never be noticed. Later, we read the words of Bishop Timothy Manning of Los Angeles: "The seed must die before it can bring forth fruit and the sower who plants in the ploughed field looks not behind to see if the seed has sprouted." And we understood his point more clearly.

CHAPTER II

UP TEPEYAC'S STEPS

Twelve hours after leaving Monterrey, drowsy as we were on a day
not two hours old, we felt both excitement and reverence upon entering Mexico City, where Our Lady of Guadalupe has reigned as
patroness since December 12, 1737. Historians record her intercession
during a terrible smallpox epidemic which raged in the country for
more than a year. Today, of course, the mother of Christ under the
title of Our Lady of Guadalupe is patroness of all the lands below the
Rio Grande. Even in the U. S. she reigns, where in 1846 the bishops
proclaimed her patroness under the title of her Immaculate Conception. Somehow, though, I felt closer to these ideas in Mexico.

Arrival time favored us. The city's helter-skelter daytime pace, con-
fusing if not harrowing to most first visitors, was hours away. Most
of her four and a half million people were asleep. When we left the
small bus terminal for the hotel nearby where our PAVLA group
was staying, only one small, aged man was in sight to help with our
luggage, his sprightly jig indicating his impatience to get on the
way and his effort to ward off the night's cold. When I mentioned
the hotel, the little man cracked a weathered smile and said, "Sí,
vamos!" and the three of us gathered our luggage for the five-minute
walk to the hotel. I wondered where the nation's youth were, a third
of whom, I had heard, do not go to school.

The Chinese night clerk at the hotel, speaking first in Spanish then
switching to English, described the last vacant room in the house and
tried to discourage us from taking it.

We told him we'd take it anyway, because our PAVLA group was lodged somewhere within those very walls, and as utter strangers to Mexico City, we didn't aim to go meandering off in the middle of the night. Realizing he could not convince us, the clerk said he'd let us have it cheaper. The reduction was from about $6 to $4.80 and, though we had been told that we should begin the bargaining in Latin American transactions, this price cut we had nothing to do with at all.

We were shown to a windowless ground floor room. The hotel's heating system which seemed to be just on the other side of the wall was hissing and thumping, and the room was hotter than July in a greenhouse. Just as we prepared to stretch out, there was a tapping on the door.

"It's the Chinaman," I said to my wife. "He wants to give *all* the pesos back!"

It was, instead, Father Mike Lies who, concerned about our arrival, had gone to the lobby to check. The Kansas priest, then on loan to Chicago PAVLA, insisted that we swap rooms with him to escape the racket and heat. We refused the generous offer.

During the 48-hour stopover in fascinating Mexico City we made repeated visits to the famed Guadalupe Shrine, even though they caused us to miss the university, the bull ring, the downtown district, La Alameda, the city's central park with the Palace of Fine Arts at its east side, and other features that should be seen as well.

From the streetside edge of the great plaza of the Guadalupe Shrine one can look beyond the impressive sandstone block and red lava brick of the basilica to Tepeyac Hill, where a chapel is seen on top marking the site where the Blessed Virgin appeared in 1531. For more than 400 years Mexicans and foreign pilgrims have labored and spent huge sums of money to provide a satisfactory shrine honoring the Blessed Mother and a sanctuary for the miraculous image. And there on the outskirts of Mexico City our PAVLA group viewed the miraculous painting on Juan Diego's mantle. The exquisite image in frames of gold, silver, and bronze hangs above the main altar, which is fashioned from Carrera marble.

Seeing humble natives edging forward on their knees toward the basilica, the stranger to Mexico is introduced somewhat overwhelmingly to a new manifestation of faith. Here are the people: many have traveled on their knees across concrete for more than a block, some cradling infants or small children in their arms. Whence comes their faith? we ask ourselves. Was it born with the miracle four centuries ago? Is it fed on the simplicity of the unschooled campesino, many of whom trek unheard of distances to pay homage to their Lady of Guadalupe? But why are the educated rich present, some of them also entering the cathedral on their knees?

The Latin faith displayed before us was not like the orderly, even somewhat casual approach observed at our great U. S. cathedrals. This sight of the witness to faith by others left us reeling.

But one must look beyond the confusion — beyond the Nahuatl Indians singing and dancing for our Lady in the plaza from morning to dusk, beyond the hawkers tugging at your coat sleeve crying out about bargains in religious goods — beyond all these to a native faith nurtured during centuries of their culture, the significance of which we could not hope to grasp in our initial exposure to it.

Lifelong Christians or not, my wife and I weren't moved to approach the main altar on our knees. To do so would have been an act of phoniness. Perhaps after three years in Peru we would possibly have been conditioned to go down the center aisle in that manner. As it happened we had no opportunity to revisit the shrine on our way back.

Hurrying back and forth between hotel and shrine (a few places seen were the cathedral and Plaza de Armas and the elegant convent school where nuns from the Benedictine convent in Atchison, Kansas, are assigned) we worked up an appetite. Despite the danger of dysentery, mid-afternoon hunger won out one day when the evening meal at the hotel still seemed far away. We ambled over to a large market near the basilica and walked among the baked goods and its wonderful aroma. Five minutes later standing on a corner in busy Mexico City we finished off the last of a half dozen sugar rolls.

The following day, February 1, at a side altar off the basilica's ornate main sanctuary, Father Stitz celebrated High Mass for the nine PVs leaving for Peru and Brazil. Privately, we made our commitments to serve God in the years ahead. It was our Mass of dedication in answer to the call for volunteers. Our group was permitted to stand on the steps inside the communion rail, singing the Mass responses, then to receive Holy Communion at the main altar rail. At the time, and it may still be so, this was a privilege denied natives or regular foreign pilgrims. We hoped that somebody had informed the many Mexican pilgrims that we were Papal Volunteers. We did not want to be mistaken for vacationing gringos from the great promised land to the north.

Outside the grand basilica we were regarded as regular *turistas*. Papal Volunteers wear no identifying emblems. Climbing the stone steps to Tepeyac Hill's chapel, we passed many pilgrims ascending on their knees. Upon leaving the chapel we paused on the steps just outside, watching a professional photographer take pictures with the chapel for backdrop. Our personal snapshot file back home recalls the time.

The biggest Guadalupe miracle of them all, of course, is encased above the main altar, the heavy, winter mantle of Juan Diego in which he carried freshly-picked flowers to the bishop from the cold, barren countryside. Pilgrims regard with awe the twisted bronze crucifix on display in the basilica. Attempts through the years to destroy the sacred painting on the *tilma* have failed, the most recent occurring on November 24, 1921. A stick of dynamite hidden in a bouquet of flowers placed on the main altar exploded. The heavy metal crucifix just below the image was twisted out of shape by the blast. Marble blocks were torn from the altar. Windows were broken in the basilica, but the precious painting, and even its glass covering, remained unscathed.

In Mexico City's traffic, when you're not at the wheel and powerless to guide your own destiny, it's best not to watch the vehicular madness ahead. Besides possibly avoiding a heart attack you will miss many unusual sights, such as that of dozens of young Mexicans in action below a viaduct, practicing the art of the matadors, one with cape and another holding sticks in imitation of horns against his forehead.

The first on-the-job Papal Volunteers we met were assigned to radio communications in a small pueblo not far from Mexico City. It was Friday, and we dined with them on roast beef. This was our introduction to eating meat on Friday and for the first time at a Mexican table we relaxed, ate heartily, and gave no thought to stomach miseries on the prowl; here we realized for the first time that one can be too finicky about eating in Latin lands, and that common sense must be one's guide.

There are certain other things to be gotten used to in Mexico: the apparel of religious, for example, who are not allowed to wear their ordinary religious dress in public: cassocks, Roman collars, or habits with rosary beads clicking at the side. Our PAVLA priests shed their collars at the border, dressing in black ties and white shirts later. We were reminded of this civil law again when we entered the convent to meet the sisters who had been in Mexico for years on assignment from their original motherhouse in Kansas.

Two nuns entered wearing blue matched skirts and suitcoats with white blouses open at the throat. Seeing nuns garbed in modern dress and with gray tinted hair done up stylishly was a shock to one who had grown up with those who sang out "yes-ter" and "no-ster" to their teachers all through the grades. Starchy linen, black folds of skirts and shawls, pink cheeks contrasting with white coifs on wintry days. . . . I had thought these styles unchangeable. Two very dedicated nuns entered dressed like business women going to an afternoon meeting!

In Mexico City we struggled to learn how to switch from dollars and dimes to pesos and centavos without taking a loss. Then again, when the taxi zoomed along the city streets, the speedometer pointing to 70 kilometers, six or seven pairs of eyes stuffed into the cab with the rest of our bodies tried to see the speed in that wild traffic as actually 45 miles per hour. On scales the needle stopped at 86 for my weight, but hurried multiplication by 2.2 (pounds per kilogram) kept the weight up there at about 189.2 pounds.

How many litres in a gallon? What size shoe do you ask for? When I eventually met the shoe need in Lima, an obliging clerk brought out a half dozen pairs of black ones. The slightly pinching pair of brushed pigskin uppers I walked out with were Peruvian size 44, the largest he had (and I thought they'd stretch a little). Back in Kansas City they would have been in the 10½ stack.

Four of us left Mexico City airport at noon on a very warm February 3rd on a Peruvian airlines prop plane; the remaining five women took off for Brazil an hour later, tightly clutching their tickets and their cumbersome portable TV they had struggled with at every checkpoint in Mexico. By the time we arrived in Lima, some 4,450 miles from Kansas City, we had had our share of buses and flying for a spell.

It was a fourteen-hour flight with stops in Honduras and Ecuador; hours whiled away with pencil and paper games, time out for eating, for napping, and for peering down upon the Central American landscape. A short way out of Mexico City excitement among the passengers mounted at the sight of majestic Popocatepetl, traditional mountain of love, its cone-shaped snow crown 17,800 feet above sea level, piercing the blue sky.

Because of religious ignorance in Latin America, poverty and suffering, shortages of priests and nuns, assaults upon the Church by the Communists, and anti-clericalism, volunteers going south to help the Church must never forget love for those members of Christ's Mystical Body, forgotten souls, who are very much in agony. Popocatepetl . . . mountain of love. Glancing back to the north, we saw the pinnacle recede into the distance. We saw it as a symbol.

A feeling persisted within us that as lay people going below the border for the Church, we were pioneering, although Catholic religious missioners have been working at strengthening and extending the faith in the New World ever since the early sixteenth century. For more than 400 years the Church has been there, waging a campaign in treacherous terrain, with civil and financial restrictions, and among unschooled natives — the latter, the result of landed gentry keeping the campesino masses under its thumb. Such mission work, however, had been carried on only by priests, nuns, and brothers.

Until the 1950's, the hierarchy and clergy in the U. S. did not openly invite or suggest that lay people with skills and zeal come forward to help. Then, the idea of a layman going to the foreign missions was rather fantastic. The role of the layman was to open his purse or perhaps to join in prayers when the missionary spirit moved the parish. Meanwhile, populations in mission lands soared. Mission religious were swamped with the neglected children of God.

In the four-engine piston plane, high over Guatemala, we struck up a conversation with a young North American couple with two small children seated across the aisle and an alarming truth came to us, a truth that in Peru was to be impressed upon us over and over as we made our rounds. The couple listened with interest as we explained about Papal Volunteers and other Catholic lay groups now leaving homes in the United States, giving up jobs, security, and other important things to go to Latin American missions. This couple had left all of this behind five years before when they became lay missioners for a gospel tract group out of Los Angeles. What really astounded them was that they were meeting Catholic lay people who were not traveling to jobs with fancy overseas salaries in the state department, not management personnel for oil companies, not Peace Corpsmen. Our motive, we told them, was sparked by faith and hope that as Papal Volunteers we could help bolster the sagging Catholic faith, as Catholic *laymen,* in Latin America.

Instead of exclaiming, perhaps, "How wonderful!" they asked what we had been waiting for. "Protestant missionaries," they said, "have been in those Catholic nations for 40 years and more!"

Weeks later we would discover firsthand that what we had believed to be a Latin Church of extreme piety and participation was actually a Church greatly neglected by too many of her native, baptized members. We also learned to our great surprise that the wife of that family across the aisle was a baptized Catholic herself. Somewhere along the way she had embraced a religion that seemed to give her greater spiritual fulfillment.

As we stretched our legs at the first stop in Tegucigalpa, Honduras, I looked off across the runways to a small cluster of Honduras air force hangars. Lined up in front were six Corsair planes made in the U. S. and used so effectively as the navy's carrier-based fighters during World War II. Now the once-sleek, swift planes, with the inverted gull-wings that folded back to save space aboard aircraft carriers, looked very old, very outdated, very slow.

I thought of the old airplanes as symbols of a hard-to-face fact. Our Church's lay mission answer to the apostolic call in the U. S. A. is as far behind the times as those vintage planes. Little Honduras, a nation with a literacy rate of only 35 percent, relying on revenue from exported bananas and coffee for a meager income, hangs on tenaciously amid a world of power pressures. In a manner of speaking, the initial contingents of U. S. lay workers in Latin lands were asked to hang on doggedly, too, until reinforcements arrived. And at this writing our Catholic lay people are, so to speak, still flying those old Corsairs in an era when supersonic passenger jets are but a few years away.

Leaving Honduras and its balmy weather, our plane roared full throttle for takeoff toward a mountain range, banking at the proper moment to follow a green valley as it strained for altitude. Some two degrees north of Guayaquil, Ecuador, the plane crossed the equator. At the moment most of the passengers slept, and no mention of the crossing was made. Next stop: equatorial, sweltering Guayaquil where we arrived in darkness, swapped unneeded Mexican pesos for about thirty cents' worth of Ecuadorian sucres with which we bought a souvenir, then resumed the flight south toward the Land of the Incas.

Peru is not only the home of famed Machu Picchu, ruins of the Inca Empire, but also the primary fishmeal producer in the world, a fact brought sharply to us via our sense of smell when we arrived at the airport outside Lima, for the wind was not off the sea that time.

As it happened, our arrivals at various points in Latin America were early in the morning. So, too, in Peru. Customs checkers, hearing each of us repeat "used clothes" and "Papal Volunteers" in our first real crack at Spanish, moved us smoothly through immigration. When we entered an almost vacant waiting room, we realized that nobody had come to meet us. We called Father Thomas F. Garrity.

"Tomorrow," he yawned into the phone. "Tomorrow you're supposed to get here!" Father Tom had got out of bed to answer his phone "en la madrugada," in the early Sunday hours of a Peruvian summer day with himself scheduled for first Mass.

Assured that we definitely were in Peru and like lost sheep at the airport, he rattled off directions, spelling out places like Balconcillo for his neighborhood and *parroquia* for his parish. We piled into an old 1937 Plymouth with flapping fenders and one headlight, confident the driver knew where the Maryknoll Fathers' parish of Our Lady of Guadalupe was located. After all, hadn't he politely replied, "Por supuesto!" "Of course!"

Normally the trip from the airport to Balconcillo takes half an hour. During rush hours fifteen minutes more are required. But an hour and a quarter on the way could mean only one thing — the cabbie was lost! And, of course, we were too.

February 4th is not a Peruvian holiday, but during our meandering through Lima's southeast neighborhoods (and that city of two million is big!) our concern about being lost was not as great as our amazement at seeing so many crowded cantinas with people spilling out of them into the streets. Peruvian music blared out across the neighborhood into the early dawn.

For a large segment of the working-class, for the unemployed who can scare up the *soles,* and for the rich, the meaning of Saturday night is pleasure, pleasure that always lasts into Sunday morning, often till long after the forenoon Mass schedules have been completed in the churches. Some will get to the evening Masses.

Frequently during the search for Balconcillo's parish the driver stopped to ask directions of reveling countrymen. Limaneans peered in at us and made comments which we didn't understand. They could have been inviting us into the cantina for a pisco sour, renowned in Peru and remembered by visitors. Maybe they were telling us Yankees to go home.

At times we were a bit frightened. Why not? We were lost, almost tongue-tied by the language barrier, and we had real doubts about the cab hanging together much longer. Finally, as the tired taxi wheeled along Avenida Mexico, and approached the intersection of Palermo, we saw the Maryknoll parish. The Taj Mahal in full moonlight could not have looked more grand!

This was our welcome to Peru! So different from the four-colored travel brochures that tell about Inca ruins, Cabo Blanco with its black marlin where Hemingway fished, Iquitos in the exciting jungle, and Peru's "fabulous capital, Lima!"

Whereas tourists spend days experiencing the excitement, Papal Volunteers have the opportunity to spend years. My wife and I would never swap the latter opportunity for the former.

CHAPTER III

IN JOHN BULL'S SHADOW

Along Main Street U. S. A. she would have been a typical teen-ager in the days when ponytail hair styling was the fad. She wore a flowery print sundress and, walking near the exquisite poinsettia blooms growing profusely on trees larger than the mulberry north of the Rio Grande, she lent beauty to beauty on that sunny Peruvian afternoon. But instead of dancing black eyes and a kindly smile, she carried a stern, troubled look with a slight hint of affected hardness. We were on a street called Coronel Inclan in the Miraflores district of Lima, and as she approached, it was obvious that she wanted to satisfy her curiosity about us.

Later, during our years in Peru, we recalled that this girl fit the description of her country's most brilliant author, Ricardo Palma (1833–1919) in his book, *Peruvian Traditions:*

> The girl was one of those beauties Lima is famous for who could have charmed the devil himself and made him cross himself and turn somersaults. She had a pair of black eyes that were like two charges of dynamite.

"Are you North Americans?" she asked in English even before a cordial "Good Day" greeting, a wonderful trait of so many Peruvians. The girl, who said her name was Adela, suspected from our universal travelers' trademark, the camera strung around my neck, and the gadget bag Mary Ellen carried, that we had not been in her country very long. After we had answered her first question, Adela continued to ask more, rather belligerently, "Why did you take a picture of my church and the wall back there," she asked. "And the

Bishop Mark K. Carroll presenting mission cross at PAVLA departure ceremony, Wichita cathedral. McCarthys were the first married volunteers in the Wichita program . . . Arriving at Our Lady of Guadalupe basilica, Mexico City, some pilgrims approach famed church on knees . . . A Mexican maiden waits to enter Guadalupe shrine and offer flowers to the Virgin and Child.

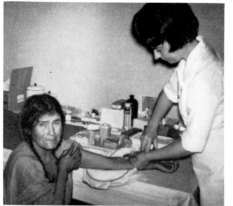

Peruvian woman in Marykno[ll] Guadalupe parish clinic, Lima, [re-]ceives injection from Mrs. McCart[?] . . . Four little Lima girls will so[on] have hot powdered milk and bre[ad] rolls to start them on their day . [. .] Outstretched hands reach for whe[at] symbolic of Peru's need as develo[p-]ing nation. Artwork is at Pampa [de] Comas, slum home for about 11[0,]000 people . . . Baptist chur[ch] in Lima's Miraflores district. Ne[w] classrooms and activity center a[re] being constructed on the left si[de] of the church.

man selling bananas and the sewer in the middle of the street without a cover?" Mary Ellen and I looked at each other in surprise, then back to the girl.

"You've been following us quite awhile, haven't you, señorita?" I said.

Yes, she had, and added that our picture taking didn't make any sense to her. Why our interest in the cream-colored stucco church she attended at the corner? It was a small but well-kept Baptist church with *Iglesia Bautista* in large block lettering over the main entrance. And why would we also, Adela wondered, be taking pictures of a high white wall containing political slogans of one of the nation's presidential candidates? Someone had crudely painted the Spanish word for rat across the name of the candidate.

We took the first opportunity to explain to her that we were not merely tourists on a whirlwind fling at her city, but that we were Papal Volunteers. Did she know about them?

"No," Adela said. But she admitted that she had been originally baptized in the Catholic faith and used to attend Mass. During Adela's high school days, new personal and spiritual interests led her into the church at the corner.

Assured that the majority of the people in the United States didn't know politicians Odria, Haya de la Torre or any other candidates, and that we weren't scheming to link anybody with anything in our picture taking, Adela relaxed somewhat, and leaned back against the wall of Bodega Gladys, the neighborhood grocery store operated by some very congenial young Chinese boys. She had studied her English in a private school and was eager to practice it. She lived in good middle-class surroundings several blocks away from where she attended church. Moments before, I had taken Mary Ellen's picture in front of a butcher shop where the fresh meat hung unrefrigerated in the doorway, with Mary Ellen posing as if she were shopping for the day's needs. Adela had rounded the corner just as the shutter snapped. We were on our first jaunt outside the British pensión, a boarding house where we were staying, and were completely fascinated by the many new sights in this, to us, completely foreign land.

"Is there anything wrong with taking a picture of your church, Señorita?" I asked. Gradually, she abandoned her defensive attitude. It was somewhat surprising, we said, in our introduction to Peru where ninety-five percent of the people are baptized Catholics, to see a flourishing Baptist church. Moreover, the new construction under way next to the church indicated expansion.

In Peru, Roman Catholicism is the official religion and is protected by the national constitution. But there are no restrictions on the activities of other religious denominations. In our days there we were to see more than a dozen religious groups hard at work for converts, some of them making recognizable gains.

Adela was an example of many of her countrymen who understand their inherited Catholic religion only as a coat, as something to be put on or taken off at will. Only the day before, Mary Ellen and I had begun attending Mass at the modernistic Santa Maria Reina church which U. S. missionaries had constructed and dedicated in 1954. The bell tower of the gringo priests' church almost casts a shadow over Adela's home. But she wasn't practicing that faith anymore.

She said she had been told that about 75 percent of their Catholic priests go around in black or white cassocks under a vow not to marry and to remain chaste yet they have their women and children. In addition, Adela gave us a long string of other popular generalities. True, some of the Latin priests have sons for altar boys, but we added that in the United States some priests abandon their vows, too. Her look was one of utter disbelief. We tried to explain that if they marry, they no longer represent the Church and her teachings. When discovered, they are allowed to serve as priests again only after renunciation of their bad conduct and reinstatement by the Church. We assured the skeptical señorita, that not only are Latin American priests who, because of handicaps such as inferior seminary training, extremely poor parishes, or utter solitude, lost in religion, but also some North American missionary priests have renounced their vows and began family life in South America.

"Priests are very human, Señorita. When you hear them say 'Pray for me,' you know they mean it. They need prayers of their own and others to strengthen them in their vocation," Mary Ellen said.

We suspected that she disallowed what she had been hearing and did not care to reason that fallen creatures among religious or laity do not constitute total condemnation of a Church 2,000 years old. As we started back to our boarding house, this young Peruvian woman in all sincerity tossed out another accusation: that the thousands of silver regalas (thin, silver-leaf medallions placed in churches near altars, statues, and religious pictures for favors granted) had to be collected annually and sent to Rome or "the Pope will order the saints in heaven to do terribly bad things to the people in Peru!"

In the United States it is customary for Catholics to send donations to the missions or light votive candles for favors received or for petitions sought. Peruvians and other Latins, on the other hand, buy silver-leaf gifts to pin near statues of Our Lady of Guadalupe, Our Lord of the Miracles, and their favorite saints. These thin medallions, called Gracias Regalas, vary greatly in size. Some are small as quarters, costing about that amount. Others are larger than pizza pies and normally are used by the wealthy. From time to time the great accumulation of these gifts necessitates their removal to allow space for others. Their periodic removal is with parishioners' approval. The metal is melted and re-formed into objects for the church, such as candle sticks, altar missal holders, frames for spiritual pictures, and the like.

A few days later we included in our first tour of Lima's religious and historical monuments a visit to the Convent of St. Dominic, where St. Rose of Lima took the robes of her order in 1606, changing her name from Isabel Flores de Oliva. Because our encounter with Adela was still a vivid memory, we were not inclined to disbelieve the weakness of the Latin American Church, which Pope John had said caused him to lose sleep at night.

There on the outside wall of the convent chapel, where people turn in off the sidewalk along Avenida Tacna, was a large poster urging the people of Lima to attend a great Christian "Crusade for Christ" led by the famed Evangelist Billy Graham. After making his way through Venezuela, Colombia, and Ecuador, Graham arrived in Peru and told the people that a large percentage of them do not attend church, or do so very irregularly, and that he wanted them to accept the Lord, to go to church regularly, to live like Christians.

There's no question that the Latins have accepted the Lord; that individualistic brand of faith among so many unschooled and literate alike seems fathomless. But Papal Volunteers and religious share Mr. Graham's concern about the large numbers who should be attending church regularly and living like Christians but are not. Thousands of Peruvians gathered in a Lima bullring to hear Billy Graham, the man who won public praise from Boston's Richard Cardinal Cushing who said that the Catholic Church should have some dynamic men like him. It could never be determined, of course, how many people flocked to the Graham prayer meeting simply to get a change from their everyday world, a place where there would be electric lights and music and happiness compared to the dull inside of a slum hut. Where the crowds form in Latin America, pickpockets gather, even in church!

We became sharply aware of how different things are amid a foreign culture flourishing on the western slopes of the Andes Mountains. Some of these differences we saw those first few days on Peruvian soil.

1) An earthquake almost shook us out of bed the third morning in town. Next morning's headlines calmly reported it as "loud but inoffensive."

2) My wallet was lifted from my side pants pocket with the greatest of ease — and success for the pickpocket.

3) We were billeted in four different lodgings during our first five nights before settling at the boarding house.

4) Without a car we learned how to walk again, and we could feel nothing but amusement at the letter from the traffic department of Kansas City, Mo., ordering me to appear immediately to pay an auto parking ticket received by the man who had purchased our car.

5) In the British atmosphere of our boarding house we were intro-
native beverages and sweets of Peru. Dinner was at eight. If you
ask me, who am used to taking evening meals at 6 o'clock, I would
duced to 5 o'clock tea and crumpets even before we sampled the

say that the delightful tea kept me from complete daily collapse before dinner.

Six days after our arrival in the sticky February heat of a Lima's midsummer, we set out along a PAVLA training course of daily spiritual suggestions and the study of Spanish and of Peruvian culture. We had entered our formation days in the field.

In and Out of the Andes, a book written by Maryknoll Sister Maria del Rey, was a part of our reading in Kansas in preparation for the missions. The section on Lima included a commentary and a photograph of the Immaculate Heart of Mary nuns from West Chester, Pa., showing their Villa Maria school for girls and convent along Avenida Arequipa in Lima. What a coincidence it was, then, to find our boarding house just a block west of them in the City of Kings!

The IHM nuns in 1922 were the first U. S. mission personnel to arrive in Peru, and their tasks long ago were necessarily pioneering ones. Home to the U. S. A., then, was not just a zippy jet flight of less than half a day; it was weeks by boat. Subsequent arrivals of U. S. missioners found IHM sisters at the docks to welcome and assist new communities over the barriers.

The new breed of lay missioners, carrying PAVLA colors, were welcomed no less enthusiastically by the Villa Maria community. Indeed, Mother Trinita and her group won an everlasting place of endearment in the hearts of our neophyte group. When they heard we were walking to daily Mass at a church almost a mile away, they offered us the opportunity to attend Mass in their chapel. After a couple of fantastically uncomfortable trips to Balconcillo from Miraflores in public buses jammed to body-crushing capacities, we were invited to make the morning trip to our Spanish classes in the sisters' school bus, which took some of their students into underdeveloped areas of the city to teach summer catechism classes. The bus passed within two blocks of our assigned Maryknoll parish. No longer were we in danger of being carried as far as a mile from our destination because of the delay in squeezing through the humanity to the front of the public bus. Peruvian bus riders, it should be said, own a special sense of humor — they have to to retain their sanity —

and they must have enjoyed the spectacle of us gringos arising to the unique challenge of alighting from the bus in one piece. Straightening disarrayed clothing once outside the packed bus was like dressing all over again to begin the new day. God bless the good IHM nuns! We had had our share of bus scrimmage when they rescued us.

Any frustrations arising from being buffeted around emotionally and physically allowed to go unchecked would soon get one down — or send one back to the states, as did happen to some. But little things served surprisingly enough as necessary morale boosters. The very British spirit expressed by the phrase "Carry on, old boy" was rubbing off on us, too, in the boarding house amid Her Majesty's subjects.

Other great morale boosters were those wonderful letters that arrived sporadically from young pupils in the grades, letters written as assignments in English as well as geography. A PV from Connecticut passed around a letter with a little girl's observation: "It must be nice to be where places in geography are!"

Yes, it was. But if the day wasn't so nice at the moment, her words made it such. Letters containing the harvest of faithful intentions of children — sums of rosaries, Masses, Holy Communions, and ejaculations — aid your spiritual welfare in the missions. They never would meet next month's car payment, but we were walking, not driving, anyway.

We wish it were possible to thank individually all the youngsters who wrote and the many, many more whose spiritual offerings came our way, as well as to thank the adults for many kindnesses to the Peruvians and Papal Volunteers. Every PV experienced a real lift from every letter. Because Church of the Magdalen parishioners in Wichita, Kansas, backed me spiritually through prayer, and materially with $70 a month, I mention the children in Msgr. George N. Schmidt's parish, those of the eighth grade praesidium of the Legion of Mary and members of Class 5B, spring of 1962, who totaled up 7,300 ejaculations and 190 Mass and Holy Communion offerings for the spiritual welfare of the Papal Volunteers — gifts which last forever.

One letter sent to PVs going to Brazil's jungles wound up with the admonition: "Don't let the alligators eat you!"

William, a pupil in an eastern school, wrote: "I am very instred in becoming a priest but I am not good in laenten." And the good sister added her postscript: "Nor English." To a teacher bound for Peru the pupil wrote: "I hope your not having a rough time with your scholars in the third grade." In Andale, Kansas, a little girl suggested: "Maybe if you had time we could write to one another a cheerful little letter." And we did.

Money furnished by the Kansas Daughters of Isabella maintained Mary Ellen in the clinic and classroom. Forty dollars from our $70 checks helped cover room and board; the balance provided the dollar a day personal spending money as arranged in the Kansas PAVLA programing. For the trip to Peru we paid our own transportation costs; the Wichita PAVLA office paid our fares home after three years' service. By way of comparison, parents of Mormon missioners pay transportation both to and from the South American mission field.

Four months were allotted us at the beginning of our Peruvian service for study before we were sent to waiting PAVLA assignments. The youth work, the clinic and classroom, and the Catholic Information Center had to wait. Trips to the post office, the corner grocery, and the drugstore for medicine introduced us to the everyday life of Lima.

As my work clippings, notes, and correspondence began heaping up on a small desk in the corner of our bedroom, I realized that I needed a file system. I asked the grocer for a small box about file drawer dimensions. He dug out a heavy cardboard box that had brought canned pork and beans from the U. S. But boxes weren't given away, not even to regular customers. "Tres soles," the young Chinese boy asked. My 12 cent file cabinet served me well for the three years.

Seated in the enclosed backyard of the boardinghouse, memorizing such Spanish puzzlers as where a person can find a restaurant nearby that is good and cheap, I was interrupted when a low-flying Peruvian air force plane droned over dropping leaflets. I retrieved one which lodged itself in the vines shading the patio.

The English overseer of the pensión, Miss Alice Brothers, helped me translate the leaflet which announced that the government had started a "giant" crusade called "Operation Food for the People" designed to bring items of necessity to the needy at low prices. The first staple on the list was rice, which was available, the leaflet stated, at any of ten stalls in the city listed on the reverse side of the sheet. At four soles a kilogram, or just less than sixteen cents for 2.2 pounds, it was a good savings.

Thanking Miss Brothers for her kind help, I stuffed the leaflet in my pocket, not really planning to buy rice, but pleased with the Spanish lesson and the observation of the passing Peruvian scene during that study period.

Carrying two wicker baskets, Miss Brothers started off to shop for the pensión's larder. Already that day she had worked her eight hour shift as nurse-in-charge at Lima's mental hospital just atop the bluffs along Avenida Aranibar overlooking the Pacific ocean. I couldn't help marveling at that woman's dedication to the infirm, dedication that has spanned her entire nursing career.

A few words about this woman, whose example of self-sacrifice was so good for the Papal Volunteers during their introduction to Peru. In 1930 Miss Brothers as a young nurse sailed from England for Peru and immediately began nursing in the mental hospital where she worked when we lived in the pensión, which she managed because she needed extra income. "Pay at the hospital always has been low," she told Mary Ellen. "The steady diet of beans and rice almost turned me back to England several times in the early days." In 1933 Miss Brothers completed her three-year contract and returned to her home quite convinced that she would never see Peru again. But there was a letter from the hospital director pleading for her return and there were thoughts of the needs of her patients now so far from her. She went back to Lima, bringing two other nurses with her. Eventually she raised a little Peruvian girl, then danced at her wedding, and over the years helped care for her children.

Gray-haired now and overworked — though she would never admit it — Miss Brothers was up early every day, off to comfort her mental patients in whatever way she could, later directing the nurse-training program, then back to the pensión and more work. Hospital patients were her first love, her reason for selfless giving, her reward. In spite of her long stay in Peru she remained thoroughly British and, along with her countrywomen, she was thrilled by the arrival of Prince Philip in Lima on his South American jaunt in February, 1962.

Whereas Miss Brothers and the English subjects attended the British Commonwealth Community's reception for the Duke of Edinburgh, curtsying and shaking his hand, Charles Shreiner, working with Catholic Relief Services in Peru, and I watched the Duke from high up in the seats of Lima's National Stadium, where he kicked the first ball in a soccer match between Peru and Chile. Because of the feeling engendered in past border wars between the two nations the game is a real grudge match. When Peru lost, 4-2, we watched excited fans set the rented seat cushions on fire and pitch them toward the field like Fourth of July pinwheels. All the whistling going on, we learned, was the Peruvian manner of booing. This same stadium two years later, on May 24, 1964, was the scene of a tremendous human stampede in which some 303 Peruvians died following a 1-0 disputed decision in a soccer match between Peru and Argentina to determine a representative for the Tokyo Olympics. No Papal Volunteers happened to be in the stadium that night.

Something interesting was always going on in the pensión or among its boarders. One evening Miss Brothers stretched her rule of never letting out rooms to people inquiring by phone and admitted two young North American men who had called. These two new boarders kept to themselves despite the efforts at friendliness made by the other boarders. The long-haired blond boy disappeared first, his partner saying that he would be back in four days after his trip to Cuzco, Machu Picchu, and the Inca ruins. Two nights later, while everyone slept, the partner slipped out bag and baggage, leaving a week's unpaid rent and also a cluster of marijuana leaves, perhaps supposing that the gift of "pot" would cover the bill. As luck would have it, one of the men had given a Kansas City address, and since we had only recently arrived from the Greater Kansas City area, we were careful to explain that they were not any of our friends from the Heart of America!

the middle of the Peruvian summer. The people revel in Fourth of
Shortly after this experience the season of Lent arrived smack in

July weather from New Year's Day until April 1, when school officially begins. The Latin American Church's lenten regulations, therefore, are less stringent in Peru where the summer social whirl is in full swing . . . fiestas, humanity in a rush for the Pacific beaches, glitter at the race track.

The fiesta next door to the pensión that began on Saturday night went right along at a merry clip well into Palm Sunday afternoon before the music stopped. That was the weekend I learned a little more about the difference between Catholics and *practicing* Catholics. It was the time, too, that I sent home for earplugs and never more was without them when "fiestas broke out" in the neighborhood.

On Palm Sunday in the nation's churches small twigs from the olive trees are sometimes substituted for palm leaves, and what a crush of women, children, and a few men to receive them! A young priest from a U. S. missionary order related how once he watched in fright as the surge of people came toward him at the sanctuary rail. He tossed the armful of palms over their heads and retreated to the sacristy. Once, during the Holy Week surge for Holy Communion the priest had to withdraw and, after assuring the people that there was enough Jesus Christ for everybody, he was able to distribute the Hosts with some semblance of order. Such incidents are hard for North Americans to believe, but they are true; fortunately, they are not the norm.

The little vacation from Spanish classes, given us during that Holy Week, allowed Mary Ellen and me the opportunity to visit some downtown Lima churches. In the Andalusian baroque-styled church of St. Francis, a beautiful large edifice begun in 1657 and completed seventeen years later, a huge purple curtain to the left of the main altar was drawn back about the time we entered, revealing a life-sized representation of Calvary. Exultations from the people in the crowded church echoed from its art-crowded walls and high ceiling. Fourteen men made an ascent of Calvary, took down the Cross and image of the Crucified Christ, and started along the side aisles, following the Way of the Cross. We were pinned by the press of humanity to the back of our pew. When the pressure began to lessen, we fled successfully by climbing over the back of the pew.

Holy week zeal is not confined to the big cities. High in Andes valley communities and in jungle clearings, religious zeal has the accumulated significance of the ages, and there are the opposite extremes. One priest told us how the town drunk in a mountain village would stay away from church all year; then, regularly on Good Friday, he would push inside with the throng and make his way to the Crucified Christ on the sanctuary steps, proclaiming that he was sent to rescue the Lord. His attempts to remove the Corpus would be thwarted by townspeople who would hustle him outside.

The Papal Volunteer, the young nun, the newly-ordained priest arriving in the mission must prepare for such experiences. Any time another shocking incident comes to light, the missioner must adjust his perspective, absorb the new lesson in Latin American religious externals, and reinforce his own motives. Spiritual aids along the PAVLA trails, besides daily Mass and Holy Communion, are a daily visit to church, monthly Day of Recollection, annual retreat, regular contact with a spiritual director, and a chapter a day from the New Testament, or passages from *The Imitation of Christ* or from other good religious books, such as *A Book of Private Prayer*, by Dom Hubert Van Zeller — books that are spiritual powerhouses on home or mission front.

One Sunday afternoon Mary Ellen and I left the boardinghouse to make our first trip alone on the ancient trolley system; across town we were to meet PV Nurse Ethel Knecht and continue on to her clinic at the Maryknoll's City of God parish. This was to be our first closeup of poverty in a large slum of 25,000 people.

By way of explanation it should be noted that poverty can be seen anywhere in Lima; it is not restricted to ghetto areas. You may, for example, walk through Balconcillo and see many attractive dwellings of working men fashioned on apartment-style lines. Yet, at the corners or behind a wall across a vacant lot, you will find absolute poverty amid some 50 to 100 people ekeing out an existence in corralons . . . places without electricity, heat, water, sanitation. In areas like the sprawling Pampa de Comas district, San Martin district, El Montón, and such, residents by the thousands are suffering abject poverty. Such areas are the barriadas. These are the large and small islands of human misery that ring the very City of Kings!

During our trip to City of God the fine summer weather caused the working class Peruvians to flock to Barranco's Pacific shore for relaxation and sunshine. Standing on the boarding platform, watching one bulging trolley after another go by and looking every bit like the Yankee tourist — sunglasses, camera slung and ready, awed by the passing parade — we were no doubt being "cased" as soft touches for the pickpockets who ride the buses and street cars plying their trade. (At the boardinghouse they had told us to put our wallets in a side pocket, to carry our wristwatches in our pockets, not to carry a purse, and not to wear earrings.)

Finally a two-car trolley only about ninety percent jammed creaked and clanged to a halt and Mary Ellen and I pushed our way on board. As we got on a little man in front of us quickly decided that he wanted to get off, so he began muscling in between us. We had been on the trolleys a couple times previously with veteran PVs, and I was concerned about any unnecessary jostling for Mary Ellen; but while we were absorbed in the little man's departure, we got bumped from behind by his teammates in the "act" of boarding. In a split second action the pickpocket team lifted my wallet from my side pocket and disappeared down the street. When I discovered the loss, we pushed back toward the exit, hoping to get off and track down the thieves, but our path was blocked by the conductor who prevented us from leaving the trolley now as it gained speed. Gone were $15 in soles and the normal collection of ID cards and personal photos.

"Oh, they'll come to the Sacred Heart badge," I told my wife, "and guilt pangs will cause them to send back the wallet and cards at least." When I repeated this to one of the Maryknoll priests, I got no comfort. He said that the Sacred Heart badge would probably be sold with the wallet and its contents and would no doubt remind the thieves to light a votive candle for the good day's work.

Not three days later I came across St. Matthew's message in Chapter 10: "Freely you have received, freely give. Do not keep gold or silver or money in your girdles, no wallet for your journey. . . ." The wallet was never returned, but I received some comfort from Matthew's words.

After this first-hand experience with pickpockets I began a press clipping file under "Pickpocket Reports," which grew to interesting proportions. A sample of some of the items follows: Cesar Pando, retired Peruvian Army general and unsuccessful 1962–1963 presidential candidate on the National Liberation Front Communistic ticket, had his wallet filched on a bus. A watch was ripped from a wrist. Another man suffered severe head injuries jumping from a trolley in pursuit. A pickpocket well-known to Lima police lost a foot in a fall as he fled from a moving trolley. UPI reported that a wave of pickpockets from Colombia had swooped in on Los Angeles. And the popular October procession in Lima, Our Lord of the Miracles, attracted pickpockets all the way from Buenos Aires and Rio.

These samples of clippings are not intended to place a critical spotlight on Peru, but in nations with low employment rates and high illiteracy, men readily resort to theft. When, at the precise moment of the elevation of the sacred Host at Mass in a Miraflores church, a briefcase was stolen from a pew, as the clipping actually described it, one realizes how acute the problem is.

One young teacher from Newark, Ohio, had been in Lima only a few days when she appeared at our apartment for a PAVLA gathering wide-eyed and crestfallen. Would somebody lend her soles to pay the taxi fare? Two young men on a bicycle had flashed by while she stood at a curb and snatched her purse. Hers was a dismal evening, indeed.

PAVLAns win and lose. I won a contest in the pensión when I turned up at the end of its week's duration with 76 fleabites to 68 for my opponent, Charlie Shreiner. From grand mansion to barriada hovel, sand fleas are pests in Lima; you can scarcely leave a taxi or a movie without a few new bites; no matter how often the mattresses are turned or the blankets sunned, the battle against them rages unabated.

Candidates considering PAVLA work should never imagine that those in the field sail blithely through three years below the border. A visiting diocesan priest, reconnoitering the field for first-hand, horse's mouth evaluations, asked during a succulent dinner — for which he later picked up the tab — if we were happy in the work.

"That's what some of the people interested in PAVLA in my diocese want to know," he added.

While Mary Ellen and I feel unequivocally that our three years in Peru provided more true happiness and personal satisfaction than any labor prior to our commitment, we would never offer an unqualified yes to such queries. You've got to take some happiness with you. You can't be fleeing unhappiness back home, hoping to swap it for only smiles and sunshine in the mission apostolate.

Work, people, foul weather, and the like can at times create unhappy moments. A project bubble bursts; a cold, hard fact of governmental red tape blocks you; a "great idea" flops! I've sat back, blood pressure skyrocketing, and mumbled to myself about a certain priest: "How did he ever make it through the seminary?" While he no doubt wondered: "How the heck did he get into PAVLA?" But everyone mushes on, and progress outpoints failure in the long run.

Working for the Holy Father's program as we were, we would on occasion be summoned by the Papal Nuncio, Archbishop Carboni, who, while we shared a bountiful dinner with him, would ask us about our work, our problems, our general welfare. At the first such meeting we picked figs in the garden of his modest-sized Chaclacayo summer residence sheltered in a green valley at a sunny 1,900-foot level of the brown Andean foothills. During our three Peruvian years Archbishop Carboni was in close touch with PAVLA and that fact made us feel closer to the call of Pope John. Since that first session I have kept in mind the Nuncio's words: "the neglected people of the world have a priority in the Church of Christ." When one realizes that more money is spent annually in the U. S. on dog and cat food than the total mission contribution of all denominations to underprivileged lands, one can see how our priority is showing like the hem of a lacy slip. And the wealthy oligarchs of every depressed nation must share much of the blame for the neglect which smothers their downtrodden countrymen.

One has but to recall the great good accomplished by the *Hope* ship, for example, to realize that relief is arriving. In our first month in Peru, the *Hope* ship dropped anchor in Callao harbor, just outside Lima, and for a week people had the opportunity to board her and inspect the medical facilities before the ship sailed for Salaverry, about 340 miles north of Lima, to devote ten months of medical help to the Peruvians. Mary Ellen was one of the medically-trained people who toured the *Hope,* which is the former *U.S.S. Consolation,* a Navy hospital ship with military service dating back to World War II. Aboard the 250-bed complex she saw those facilities which were used to treat more than 100,000 patients in the first five years of the ship's operations around the world. *Hope's* founder and president, Dr. William B. Walsh, was named a commander in the Peruvian Order of Daniel A. Carrion. Young Carrion was a medical student credited with the first effective research in Oroya fever, also known as Carrion's disease in Peru. The skin infection accompanied by fever is endemic to the Peruvian Andes and the young medical student, during his research, contracted it and died.

During the four months' training session, while we were housed in the pensión, we were given a closer perspective of the Peruvian social welfare, religious, economic, education, and political scene, at the same time forming notions as to how we would fit into this complex picture in order to contribute what little we could.

One day in early June of 1962 we were sent out to our jobs and given the opportunity to try.

1441820

CHAPTER IV

THOSE NUNS UPSTAIRS

Forty days after Easter of 1962, Mary Ellen and I had just completed one of the easiest and strangest moves in our lives. We were sitting on the floor in the small bare dining room of a modern, two-story residence that unfortunately had no heating plant, although heat during Lima's misty chill winters is almost as vital as it is in Minnesota. Several rooms on the first floor of the house would be our Peruvian home for some months to come. We had brought with us only a couple of bulging suitcases and an army-surplus duffle bag, containing all our possessions in Peru.

After Francisco Pizarro and his conquistadors overran Peru and founded Lima in 1535, the Spaniards sent back gold, silver, and copper-laden galleons to Charles V and the phrase "It's worth a Peru." Tyrant viceroys came in to exploit the vanquished Incas. They carried mandates from the crown to rule the new possession, New Castile. The iron fist rule of the long succession of oligarchs has only in the past decade begun to ease in the face of increasing demands of the people for their human rights.

Four hundred years after Pizarro the phrase "Vale un Peru! — It's worth a Peru!" had lost its meaning. Indeed, just being in Peru represented a material loss to Papal Volunteers. But another phrase, a real slogan, took on significance for us. It was "Peru en marcha! — Peru on the march!" We hoped that our contribution to Peru's march could be measured in some gains in the standard of living, some gains in the Peruvians' concern for spirituality. We would take home with us no Peruvian gold. But we did hope and pray to return with a treasure in our hearts.

In our temporarily adopted land we harbored these thoughts while seeking to adjust to the frugality of the moment. In the cupboard of the house we had just moved into we found dishes and silverware for three place settings and a small assortment of pots and pans. But there on the floor with a Kansas City newspaper for a table cloth underneath the plates we enjoyed our supper prepared on two hot plates borrowed from Father Garrity's Maryknoll parish of Our Lady of Guadalupe. Our fare was hard-boiled eggs, hamburgers with ketchup, bread, Colombian coffee for Mary Ellen, tea for me. For dessert, each of us had a Peruvian "Sublime" chocolate bar, an item bought for about 12 cents in a store resembling a supermarket at home.

More than anything else before we left Kansas, the thought of where we would live in Peru seemed to be of greatest concern to us: a private home with running water, shared apartment, a private bath, a patch of lawn . . . ? We read and heard about Lima's slums. We saw the pictures. Would we live there?

This was our answer: We were settling ourselves in a place where any man would have least expected to live . . . in a convent for nuns. On Ascension Thursday we moved into four rooms on the first floor of a house the second floor of which was occupied by four Canadian nuns. The home belonged to a Canadian Franciscan order whose priests and brothers were running St. Anthony of Padua parish a half block away along Avenida San Felipe. Three of the sisters taught at the Franciscans' grade school; the fourth sister, fluent in English, French, and German, and busy adding Spanish to her list, kept house.

Parish and convent were located in a good neighborhood. The boulevard in front with its red cannas, well-kept hedges and grass, was maintained by laborers from the park department. But three blocks in either direction from that boulevard destitute people lived in crumbling buildings that had once stabled race horses. Happily, reasonably-priced high rise rental apartments had replaced the stables before we left Peru and the race-track had been rebuilt in the plushier, newer Montericco district.

In such a pleasant neighborhood and dwelling thoughts about mission austerity arose. There were lay volunteers in the PAVLA program, Peace Corps, and other groups who insisted on living in the poverty-stricken areas from the beginning of their assignments though at times they were not welcome in the squalid neighborhood, and always their health was in danger. As a result, some returned home in poor health. Some of the young women were accosted by shiftless men in those slums. Some moved to better neighborhoods.

Considering our situation we were not of the mind to tell directors where we wanted to live. We found that they did not believe in putting us in the slums. And indeed, according to the Papal Nuncio, lay volunteers are not to feel that they came to Latin America to work, mingle, and live among only the very indigent, illiterate people and that people outside the slums might be disregarded in the general re-establishment of the Church.

"If anyone here believes that he comes only to work with the poor and is not concerned with the spiritual uplifting of people in the working classes, the middle class, or the wealthy while he is in this nation, I would want him to leave immediately," Archbishop Romolo Carboni said during one of the occasional sessions we spent with him.

After a few days, essential furnishings were added to the apartment. A small stove with an oven replaced the hot plates. The oven never did work, however, and the man who said he was coming to repair it hadn't arrived when we left — and probably hasn't come yet. Knowing that our quarters in the convent would be temporary, we made out with the things we had: a small table and four chairs brought from the boardinghouse where we used to live; two stuffed chairs and a divan from the Franciscans; a bed which we bought after a couple of checks arrived for articles I had sold. A portable TV which might have aided our grasp of Spanish was removed to the school.

Television was not a part of our diversion during our three years in Peru. It had been introduced to Lima residents in 1958 and was but four years old when we arrived.

What surprised us was that in most slum areas ringing Lima (and larger coastal cities of Arequipa, Trujillo, Chimbote, and Ica) TV antennae could be seen. A family would put itself in debt for a TV set, then invite neighbors into the home (where essential items were lacking) to watch programs, charging the outsiders from four to eight cents per person for watching. In 1963, a year set aside especially to combat illiteracy, the government placed TV sets in certain homes where occupants would agree to bring neighbors in for government-sponsored educational programs and classes. For their cooperation, after a certain period of time, the occupants would be given the sets.

Television has become the addiction in Peru that it is in our land. Viewers eagerly watch the Lone Ranger series, with Tonto speaking Spanish. In fact, we attended one CFM meeting where ten couples spent most of the session deciding ways to regulate TV time for their children and to determine what cautions should be used in selecting programs fit for children. Who would have expected this problem in the missions?

Very soon we came to know the nuns as good neighbors, good fellow workers, and women who when they prayed, prayed hard and when they played, played hard.

During the first months in the house with the sisters above us Mary Ellen rode a bus daily to her Balconcillo parish clinic work. Meanwhile, I boarded a vintage bus, which for thirty minutes wheezed along the Jesus Leal route on its way downtown, if en route a rod didn't poke through the motor block or a tire go flat. There were new buses in Lima and there were relics. Depending upon the neighborhood where the lines operated, you got either a fancy bus or a wheezer. The evening Mary Ellen returned from the clinic later than usual, a front wheel had fallen off her bus as it rounded a corner ten bocks away. She walked home happy there were no injuries.

Automobiles for ready use were a facility most Papal Volunteers in Peru did without. In a parish without public transportation, cars had often to be borrowed. Invariably, missioners were generous about lending their cars, but of course it became rather sticky business having to go around borrowing them. The availability of a car, however, meant a person could get a half dozen jobs done in a morning; by public transportation or walking he'd be lucky to keep three appointments, a factor which over the years found us slipping into *mañana* habits about work that could have easily been done on the same day with proper transportation.

Bus riding became a habit. The first Sunday afternoon after we moved into the convent, we boarded No. 28 in front of the house simply to ride to the end of the line and back to see more of Lima. The line's end was just behind the huge major market near downtown Lima where the big garbage dump began. Most of the market refuse collected there and people came to pick it over and over again. Stepping gingerly in Sunday clothes to a bus making the return trip, we saw extremes of human degradation. About a dozen men and women were scattered along the adobe wall asleep in the last hours of sun, which soon would be clouded over for most of the winter. Some of the men had bottles snug in the crook of their arms. Bad odors of filth abounded. As we picked our way along, people stared, obviously wondering what we gringos in clean clothing were doing in their realm of misery. They had a right to wonder and the experience shocked us profoundly. It was just before elections, a time when excitable people were restive to begin with, fidgeting about, expecting something to happen (like the military coup the following month). We overheard the comments of some of the idlers about us. We were looked upon only as intruders, as Sunday sightseers.

That night a woman called upon us to ask if we might be able to help her daughter polish her English, in which she had had some private schooling. She was working in an airlines office where English, as well as Spanish, was necessary. Mary Ellen undertook to teach her nights. In several weeks she was instructing the girl as much in Catholic principles as in English. The young woman was dating a non-Catholic young man from Germany, and was attending the Catholic and the Lutheran church with him on alternate Sundays. Her mother went to Mass almost daily. The father, who had spent five years working in the U. S., didn't go to church.

Mary Ellen taught English to Luisa and at the same time picked up more Spanish for herself, until her substitute kindergarten teaching assignment became so involved there was no time for night classes.

During this period I learned that for a North American to cut grass and trim the hedges around a house in Lima was unthinkable to some proper Peruvians. Luisa's father told me so one Saturday afternoon as he walked along San Felipe.

"Hey, what are you doing there?" he asked.

"Trimming the hedge."

"You shouldn't be doing that. That's for the jardinero. How do you say that in English?"

"Gardener. Something you don't think about on $1 a day mission pay. Besides, Arturo, you remember how most people back in my home land take care of their own yards, don't you? This is good exercise."

Arturo wasn't convinced, but he changed the subject anyway, slipping into some American slang.

"Where's your old lady?" he asked.

"Mary Ellen's in the house doing laundry." I couldn't forget that! Every Saturday afternoon I carried 14 pails of hot water from our downstairs shower to the nuns' upstairs wringer-type washing machine.

"Tell her," Arturo continued, "that my old lady bought two hearts this morning in the market and we'll have the anticucho barbecue tomorrow evening. With the four of us and you two there'll be six. We've got enough heart for 12 people. Ask some of your friends to come over here tomorrow night."

Anticucho cookouts remain as tasteful and pleasant memories of Peru, the anticucho being to the Peruvian what a hotdog is to a North American. The meat is usually of beef heart, although fish, liver, or beef can be used, sliced into bite-sized chunks, then marinated overnight in a special spicy sauce. These flavorful chunks are impaled on thin, bamboo skewers, four or five chunks to a stick, then placed on the grill.

Dick Cullina, a Papal Volunteer from Hartford, Conn., helped with the anticuchos that Sunday night. Later, when only PVs were in the apartment, he told us about his work with Santiago, who hadn't been to confession in seven years, and Dick was making great progress in getting the lapsed Catholic to return to the sacraments. Dick added the details.

"Finally," Dick said, "the man decided he'd like to go to confession to one of the North American priests. I gave him a slip of paper containing the Ten Commandments and an examination of conscience, sent him into another room, told him to check it carefully. When he was ready, we'd go see Father George. Ten minutes later he stuck his head out the door, looking really worried and said: 'I did some things that aren't on the list.' "

Dick finally got him back to the sacraments, and we were present at the baptism of his son before the couple returned to the mountains. Sometime later came the sad news that his son died just before the age of six months.

All Peruvians, practicing Catholics or not, spoke with great reverence of Blessed Martin de Porres, the humble Dominican lay brother who was to become the Church's first mulatto saint. His father, of Spanish nobility, took a Panamanian mistress. Martin was born in Lima, December 9, 1579. On May 6, 1962, while Peruvian airplanes flew low over Lima and crewmen threw out thousands of leaflets containing his picture and a brief life sketch, canonization ceremonies for San Martin de Porres were being held in Vatican City. Peru's newly appointed cardinal, Juan Landazuri Ricketts, was among the jubilant Peruvians in attendance.

Going about his menial tasks of buying food in the markets, sweeping in the cloister, and being whispered about as a man to whom miraculous events had been attributed, Martin de Porres was chastized by his superiors for giving away to the poor on the streets food bought for the monastery.

We, living below the convent, were to learn firsthand 383 years later in the mulatto's backyard about God's poor. Beggars making daily rounds for food or clothing only rang the upstairs bell until they became aware of tenants on the first floor. Then our bell began ringing. The first time I answered, an unkempt middle-aged man stood at the door asking for food. Why couldn't it have been an indigent mother with children instead? Because the man before me, fully expecting a nun to answer, was mildly shocked when he found a man answering the convent door. Before I replied yes or no or maybe to his plea for food, I tried to get the point across that my wife and I lived on the first floor. My wife, I stressed, was not a nun nor was I a priest.

The next night the same man returned to beg for food and thanked me with a loud clear "Gracias, Padre!" I closed the door on his many-gestured promises that he would ask St. Francis of Assisi to bless us always and our home.

Before long we were to see many, many children and adults, too, reaching out daily for bread rolls and powdered milk in many barriadas and corralons.

Everyday Mary Ellen walked the ten blocks from the bus line to the clinic. Half of that distance was in a questionable neighborhood, so questionable, that one night when we asked the grocer how to get to a certain theater he refused to tell, saying we shouldn't be walking there at night. The movie theater, we learned later, was a block south of the route Mary Ellen took on foot to Balconcillo. The movies shown at neighborhood theaters were old movies from the U. S. with Spanish subtitles with the prices such — sixteen to twenty cents — as we could afford occasionally. Downtown Lima prices ranged around a U. S. dollar for pictures that were shown there almost as soon as in the states.

The June 10th presidential election approached, and campaigning was at fever pitch. Streets were alive with great demonstrations more vigorous, we were told, than any in Peruvian history. Seven candidates, a Communist (National Liberation Front) member among them, vied for occupancy of the palace, built in 1938 for two million dollars and situated on the north rim of Plaza de Armas which was laid out by Pizarro in 1535.

Mary Ellen returned one day and said that a man had begun saying "Buenos Dias, Señorita" to her the past few days. As lay missioners Mary Ellen believed that we shouldn't be aloof among the very people we were to work with in our assignments. She felt that our Papal Volunteer work should be known; and she explained to the man, who said how marvelous it was that North Americans came to his land to help. But when he asked her if she had ever seen the horse races at Hipodromo de Montericco, we decided that this gent in working man's clothes, about 55 years old and carrying a few carpenter's tools, should be checked out in detail.

He was nowhere to be seen the following day when I walked along with her, but he again greeted her a day or two later and asked if her husband thought he was bothering her. She said no, but the next morning I met him. During our short conversation I mentioned that our office worked close with the PIP, which in Peru means Peruvian Police Investigators and is comparable to our FBI. Mary Ellen saw him no longer. Some of the PIP's best have received diplomas from J. Edgar Hoover.

Lima's drizzly, chilly winter begins in late May and continues until mid-December. Where Lima and Callao, the harbor city, sprawl along the semi-arid Pacific ocean shore, any rain at all is front-page news. But in winter there is a constant overcast, called the "garua," a Scottish mist as Europeans named it years ago. When the winter sun does break through, youngsters in school will look up from their workbooks and shout "El Sol! El Sol!," and rooms buzz with excitement.

The "garua" rolls in under the doors, around the window casings and turns the house into an extremely uncomfortable place. Things become cold to the touch; mildew forms on clothes in the closet. I bought two flannel warmup suits: one blue, the other maroon; and after supper Mary Ellen and I would sit around looking as though ready for a track meet. We would wrap ourselves in blankets as we passed the evening, trying to study, type, or just to forget about the first winter in Lima. We retired to a bed with damp blankets, and in the morning put on damp clothes. Colds and congestion were the season's rule.

One morning we awoke to read in *La Prensa* that military officers had taken over the nation's government in a relatively peaceful revolution. The June election had been over for a month and 18 days but yet no presidential winner was declared. Someone had claimed fraud, and the election was voided. We had not been in the nation six months and whether or not we would be allowed to stay was anyone's guess at the moment. But, as I looked from the window, out upon Avenida San Felipe, my spirits soared — seeing a blue truck with the familiar red circle on the side bearing the name Sears Roebuck. If Sears was open for business and making deliveries, the nation couldn't have gone completely to pieces.

Front-page articles told how President Prado was confronted about

3 A.M. in the palace by Colonel Gonzalo Briceño who with the guns of his tanks pointed at the palace gates from Plaza de Armas, said: "Mr. President. I have orders to make you my prisoner!"

With that Peru's leader was arrested and imprisoned aboard a navy vessel off Callao harbor. The suitcase full of money in the palace, which the press reported to be the intended payoff to thwart the coup, had not served its purpose.

Concerned about the seriousness of the moment, I tried to imagine the situation if ever military men went into the White House, hustled the President out as their prisoner, then took over leadership of our nation. Although it was a frightening Peruvian fact, in view of the possible consequences, the passing Sears' truck did lend some assurance that a degree of serenity prevailed in downtown Lima that morning. I phoned the Maryknoll priests who told me that so far as they could find out the city was quiet. Water and electricity were still available in homes. Bus service was normal. Neighborhood stores were opening. Apparently, it would be safe to venture out.

I accompanied Mary Ellen to work, then continued downtown to my assignment. Across from the president's palace, the House of Pizarro, groups of civilian men milled around in Plaza de Armas, mostly watching the palace — a quiet, curious crowd. Tanks that had rumbled through the streets during early morning hours were gone. Extra military personnel were seen in the vicinity of the palace. The Civil Guardsmen wore helmets, not cloth caps. Little detachments of them, usually with an officer in charge talking into a walkie-talkie, passed at double time, ostensibly taking the pulse of crowds gathering here or there. The military coup naturally was the main topic.

The city was free of violence until nightfall, when students left their classes, when offices and shops closed, and the Peruvians gathered in clusters to discuss the new government. For them it meant no constitutional guarantees, Congress had been dissolved; there was no Chamber of Deputies or Cabinet, and of course, Peruvians wondered as to the whereabouts of President Prado. They were under the thumb of the military.

When reports of the junta takeover reached U. S. newspapers and television screens, scenes of overturned cars and buses burning in the streets were shown. These were isolated incidents, but our families and friends naturally concluded that we were in plenty of danger!

However, no worldwide press photographers or on-the-spot commentators found their way to a small, backyard convent patio where a planned anticucho barbecue took place as scheduled, turning out as a little United Nations gathering in the process. In our group were Papal Volunteers, Canadian nuns, a young couple from Switzerland doing business in Peru, a Frenchman attending college, two Spanish lay volunteers, Arturo's Peruvian family, and a man from Ecuador, who kept silent about the Peru-Ecuador border dispute.

When 9 P.M. lights-out time came for the nuns upstairs, they had already returned, read their night office, and retired, but Brother Claver Carney, stationed with Maryknoll personnel in high Andean missions around Lake Titicaca, suggested singing "Good Night, Sisters" softly and respectfully as a serenade. Next morning Mary Ellen and I sheepishly met the sisters on the way to Mass. Their superior expressed delight in the name of the community with the thoughtful goodnight song.

On other occasions we wondered if the nuns really understood us. Mary Ellen and I had just sat down to an early supper, when we discovered a little white dog, frightened but friendly and certainly a stranger to us, beneath the table curled up against the wall. Only days before a side door leading into the vacant carport had been left open. While the nuns did yard work, a dog had strayed in. So, out went this friendly little dog now from beneath our table.

Not two minutes after the dog had been "excused" from our apartment, Sister Veronica came down the back stairs calling: "Reina! Reina!"

"Oh, oh!" I moaned, backing away from the table.

Yes, Sister Veronica said, a little white dog belonging to a woman visiting upstairs was missing. Queenie, or Reina, had slipped down the back steps into our apartment! Leaving Mary Ellen to explain to the sisters, I took off to look for Queenie as the liver turned cold on my plate. Meeting the school janitor, I explained the situation, giving him name and color. He went in one direction and I, in the other. Evening shadows gathered. "Reina! Reina! Here Reina!" It was the first time I had ever called a dog in Spanish and I would have been delighted to hear a bark in any language leading up to a cheery reunion.

Circling to the north, I covered some eight blocks — giving up only after darkness settled down — hoping that the janitor had better luck or that Reina had returned to the convent.

The janitor had had no luck either; Reina didn't come home — like Lassie. And to make things worse, the owner told us that her dog could dance. Reina's owner returned home without her dog. Two weeks later we learned that Reina had not yet been found. To this day I feel that if ever somebody wanted a Yankee to leave Latin America, it must have been the dog's mistress. I have not forgotten either that the little white dog could dance!

Jollier moments returned. When the word was out that another sister was due to arrive from Canada, we wondered if she'd be moving into the rear downstairs room. If so, our days in the convent were numbered; however, space was provided upstairs for Sister Jane.

The nuns' delight was to accord Sister Jane the proper convent initiation, a standing bit of humor with the veterans upstairs. Before sitting down to the first meal with the new sister, one nun had gone unnoticed to the backyard banana tree that never grew a banana in its life, and placed securely amid the swaying fronds a fine, yellow hand of bananas purchased at the market. As dessert time approached, sister superior asked excitedly if the sisters would prefer the bananas "just ripe today in the garden" to the pudding. The new sister, thrilled at the thought of having bananas right off the tree, joined the chorus of voices preferring bananas to pudding. If she was thrilled at the prospect of having home-grown bananas, she was overwhelmed when she was told she could pick the bananas herself. She was assured that she would find them right in front of the first frond. Sister Jane returned with the bananas as the convent upstairs was swept with laughter and applause. A couple of rounds of lively square dancing followed. Below we marveled at the strength of Peruvian plaster.

On a Pueblo Libre street near the home there was a smile for anyone at a fix-it shop where a sign over the door read: "We don't know nothing, but we fix everything!" You look at the sign, then at the man seated in the doorway, tapping, tapping on the bottom of a kettle to make it serve some housekeeper another year. There is an exchange of friendliness recognized the world over — a smile. Before we moved from the neighborhood, the man had repaired one wooden, hand-made ironing board, a clock, an electric heater, and had mended a leatherette brief case that I carried daily on the downtown beat. Peruvians have good humor in the main, like the taxi driver who had the sign painted on the back of his 1929 Model A Ford: "I am old, but don't tell me."

The supermarket was ten city blocks from our apartment. As you carried large brown bags filled with the week's groceries, a feeling that you well might be home on a Saturday morning in the suburbs vanished as you passed the parking lot and continued walking instead almost a mile to your home. We walked that grocery trip twice, no more. It wasn't the distance, and it wasn't the weight, because canned goods were too expensive for PV budgets.

What really stopped our weekly walk along streets with armloads of groceries were the poor children of Peru who played outside gated walls that hid their corralon misery from the view of better-off citizens. They remembered only the slim pickin's of the meal just past — so the sight of North Americans walking along with a week's groceries was fantastic. They looked like . . . well, how ragged, dirt-caked kids look when you walk near them with food. We wilted. Thereafter we took a cab home setting aside ten soles (about 40 cents) for cab fare.

While we still were neighbors of the nuns, Marilyn Monroe took her overdose of barbiturates, death coming to the glamor girl whose own childhood had recollection of tough times. Although the sisters read the same morning edition as we did, they never did mention her death to us. *Expreso*, the sensational tabloid, carried a screaming inch-high headline "Marilyn Elects to Sleep Forever." The subhead continued: "Nude and with a Hand on the Telephone: 'Hello? Is God There?'" In our Peruvian adjustment we were to observe some strange mixing of religion with the seamy side of life. In another version of this curious mixture one stage play included a half dozen scantily-clad chorines doing a number with a male member of the cast dressed in the brown robes and sandals of a Franciscan friar dancing about on the boards. This play lasted only as long as it took to get a picture of the dance in the newspaper. Then the boom lowered.

One half-page advertisement showed a young *señorita* kneeling in the confessional, asking if it was all right to use "Bikini" Suntan Lotion. Our Catholic Information Center joined forces with Peruvians to stop that ad.

Off duty, answering the downstairs doorbell afforded me some interesting surprises. One evening when I answered the bell, two impeccably dressed young men greeted me. They came to bring their message about the Mormon religion, but when they learned we, too, were North American, we just talked. Both men (there were about 180 men and 30 women from the U. S. western states working in Colombia, Ecuador, Peru, and northern Chile) were surprised we, too, were missionaries. The night they were at our door there were only about 150 Catholic lay workers from North America in all of the Latin America. At the end of our three years some 375 Catholic laity, representing PAVLA, Grail, Lay Mission Helpers, Catholics for Latin America, and several other groups were in the field.

Another time when I answered the bell, I was handed a bag of groceries by a young Peruvian who ran off with nary an explanation. We thought word had got around about the volunteers' low wages. I asked my wife, wondering if perhaps she had ordered something for delivery, but she hadn't. The brown bag contained margarine, bread, soap, cocoa, seasoning, spaghetti, vanilla pudding, and fried corn curls. Neither one of us was having a birthday. The mystery was solved by a note from the store manager explaining that he wanted us to check the quality and freshness of all the FREE SAMPLES and then drop around to visit the supermarket that had just opened nearby.

One youthful doorbell ringer talked so fast that I went inside and asked Mary Ellen if she wanted to buy any watermelon. No? That was fine; for the boy really was trying to buy old bottles. Don't worry about the language. You pick it up easily on the streets!

While we were having a meal of peanut butter sandwiches one evening, two men in black suits and Roman collars turned up, just having arrived in Lima after a flying-boat trip along the Amazon river from Brazil. As they helped with the sandwiches, they told us details of their work along the great river mission stations with Mary Ellen's brother, Father John Moffitt, a Redemptorist priest. The men returned the next night for a dinner of spaghetti and meatballs, my wife's overseas specialty.

CHAPTER V

LIMA . . . "THE CITY THAT TALKS"

"I believe that here, Lord, of all the other places
in the world, is where you want me to be."

— Dom Hubert Von Zeller

In the early days of World War II, Dr. Manuel Prado, moving confidently through his first full six-year term as Peru's president, and Franklin Delano Roosevelt linked their nations by pact with the Allied effort to defeat the Axis powers. Some of Peru's young men came north to serve in branches of U. S. military units. During those days the combined populations of the nation's capital, Lima, and the nearby port city of Callao totaled only 400,000 people.

Twenty years later, with President Prado back in office for his second term, Peru again was aligned closely with the U. S. A. The link this time was not against a military enemy but rather the crash-type Alliance for Progress program, a peaceful hemispheric crusade shaping ways of rolling back Latin America's tide of human misery.

In those two decades the world's population increase was reflected in the growth of the Lima-Callao population alone, which skyrocketed to almost two million people. Five hundred thousand of them, in 1962, were crowded into shantytowns; some of which had more than 100,000 inhabitants, and others scarcely more than 20 families clustered in squalor behind an adobe wall. In between were slums of assorted sizes.

At the government level the two nations worked on social welfare programs to lessen the misery. From a church approach at our PAVLA level in Lima, Mary Ellen and I worked to become elements of this

51

humanitarian, Christian chain of events linking our nations anew.

Lima was named the City of Kings by Francisco Pizarro when his conquistadors founded it just 43 years after Columbus arrived in the New World. She seemed anything but that to us because of the half million people existing in some 150 barriadas and corralons ringing the city, people who in only the past few years had experienced some relief in those burgeoning islands of social neglect.

Lima occupies about twenty miles of Peru's 1,400-mile Pacific ocean front, located fairly equidistant between Ecuador on the north and Chile down south. The Rimac river, roaring out of the Andean foothills, bisects the city. The word "Lima" is said to come from the Quechua Indian dialect and means "the city that talks." We found her not so much the city "that talks" as a city "talked about" — in Washington, D. C., Peking, and Moscow, for instance, where the world's power politics are centered; in Vatican City where peace talk is often repeated; in the offices of the Papal Volunteers; and in centers of many religious denominations and world work camp groups that send personnel within her boundaries. Lima is talked about by tourists, too, but unfortunately not many tourists see the anguish in the city's crowded quarters.

Like water surging westward in the Rimac channel and in 56 other Peruvian rivers, large and small, rolling off the Andean spine, many Peruvians from the hills and jungle have left their unproductive communities for big cities, Lima getting the bulk of them. Others, such as Arequipa, Ica, Trujillo, Chimbote, and Chiclayo, feel the population swell also. Much of the poverty is to be found along the banks of the Rimac River where the people from outside Lima have squatted to be near one of life's great essentials — water.

In 1958 seven miles north of Lima's Plaza San Martin there was only an empty, arid wasteland called Pampa de Comas stretching east to the brown foothills from lush, green, profitable hacienda fields. Five years later, more than 100,000 impoverished Peruvians had settled there. We stood with Father Andres Godin, a French-Canadian Oblate of Mary Immaculate missioner, and viewed the panorama of nondescript homes and dusty streets. From Our Lady of Peace parish he and his aides including a handful of Papal Volunteers bring some

A tank truck brings vital water to Pampa de Comas, north of Lima . . . A vintage carriage brings a new foreign ambassador, with his credentials, to President Belaunde, in front of Peru's presidential palace . . . A Peruvian child drinks warm milk and soon shares her bread-roll bits with her puppy . . . Outside Lima's massive cathedral on Plaza de Armas a police-man awaits throngs expected for a special feastday Mass.

Boys from makeshift homes (seen below) have just received First Communion in Maryknoll's Guadalupe parish, Lima . . . Juan Pizarro, whose Spanish Conquistadors overran Inca masses in the 1530s, immortalized in bronze off Lima's Plaza de Armas . . . Houses crowded onto Lima hillside lack electricity, water, and heat; happily there's room for fulbito (miniature soccer) on basketball court.

Gigantic last of October annual procession of Our Lord of the Miracles draws tens of thousands imploring protection from Peru's frequent earthquakes. In Lima's Plaza de Armas some 60,000 persons venerate the Calvary painting . . . Peruvian student nurses return from HOPE hospital ship berthed at Lima's port of Callao, before duty at Salaverry. Fish-meal exports, important Peruvian industry, are seen.

They still smile despite incredible poverty. These forgotten ones help write a Papal Volunteer's "paycheck." . . . Interest centers around nail-clipper demonstration; author chats with young Lima girls while on photo-story assignment at City of God, south of Lima . . . In Lima's City of God settlement, children watch sparks fly as the housewife's knife is sharpened . . . Archbishop Romolo Carboni, congenial Papal Nuncio to Peru, greets Papal Volunteers.

little happiness into the lives of these people through the community center, the health clinic, the boys' and girls' industrial schools. Some of the projects are aided by Ford Foundation grants. What is puzzling is that a secretary in a downtown office, owning a car, had heard of the sprawling mass of Comas neglect but had not yet actually seen it when we talked. She is a woman of good heart but she admitted she would not go there for fear of having stones thrown at her car or maybe even have it stolen from her. Indeed, she is aware of her nation's social injustice. Gradually, perhaps, she and others will follow paths toward bringing aid to their countrymen.

Lima is a place where grand damas raised money to help equip a pavilion in the large Archbishop Loayza public hospital while we were there by promoting a lusty Italian movie. The film, *Bikinis on the Beach,* packed them in for the benevolent cause. The hospital was named after an early Peruvian archbishop. This incongruity is baffling.

In the conference rooms of the presidential palace, the Senate and the Chamber of Deputies, dedicated Peruvian statesmen labor to shape colonization programs for the nation's potentially productive yet uninhabited zones to solve Lima's (and the other larger cities') riddle of unemployment, slum housing, poor health, and illiteracy.

Going about my job, I found Lima a city of violent contrasts. One vivid memory among many goes back to one morning when we were with a group of newly-arrived Papal Volunteers, escorting them to the tastefully-appointed reception room of Cardinal Landazuri. The glances of the new arrivals swept the room with its large paintings of former church leaders and the elegant throne for formal occasions, and we felt with them the thrill of the moment — a chat with the Cardinal. That afternoon with camera and note pad, I watched as Cardinal Landazuri arrived in a slum (he is no stranger to them) standing in the back of an old pickup truck waving to the ill-clothed, ill-fed crowd. He'd come into the *Primero de Mayo barriada* to bless another *Centro de Superación* community center where people could go for emergency family care, and to learn basic trades.

"Viva El Cardenal! Viva El Cardenal!" shouted people pressing toward the passing truck. The Church's Primate in Peru had come to them. Someone, indeed, did care.

Clustered at the entrance to the center, which actually was a storage room somewhat refurbished, were a half dozen women entirely out of their social class as their dresses and finery indicated. But they were, nonetheless, women concerned about a solution to Lima's blight. As members of international B'nai B'rith's local branch they stood with their ambassador to Peru from the Republic of Israel awaiting the benediction. These Jewish women had financed the project and donated hours of labor preparing the center.

The dedication ended. We came out into the gathering dusk and greeted Cardinal Landazuri as he was being assisted into the back of the pickup truck, returning him to the fringe of the slum where his own auto awaited. The dust settled. People slowly returned to their makeshift dwellings. Some came back to the center to savor anew something good that had been added to their little stake in the world. I stood in the parched roadway and saw in the distance the huge electrical sign on top of the Crillon Hotel in downtown Lima. Below the sign in the plush hotel's dozen floors were wealth, abundance, glamor vying for tomorrow's society headlines, sumptuous food, Turkish baths, clean beds, swimming pool, television, *El Galeon* cocktail lounge . . . whatever money could buy man in pursuit of happiness, real or artificial. On C.I.C. or PAVLA assignment I had been a Crillon visitor. Now, in the dust of one of Lima's most dismal neighborhoods, *Primero de Mayo,* the awful contrast momentarily sickened me. Neglect at my side, excesses of luxury in the distance. But amid them had come a member of the Sacred College of Cardinals and Israel's most influential representative in Peru. In gathering shadows a bright burst of abstract love and sincere concern seemed to light *Primero de Mayo* slum where there were no lights, no tap water, no heat. Beneath the Crillon hotel sign chefs in immaculate uniforms busily prepared multi-course dinners in another world. Here, grubby children, long without baths, swarmed around as Father Garrity and I walked toward his car and drove out of the belly of the slums ringing the city.

In present-day Lima one out of every four people lives in a slum. Clear and present social injustices now concern not only the helpless throngs consigned to those slums, but they concern every Limanean from the slum dwellers themselves right up to the doors of the palace. Indeed, President Belaunde has taken the lead in the growing crusade against illiteracy, poverty, and human deprivation.

At one point while in Peru we were taken to task in a letter by a woman from the United States for writing "only about the poverty and misery in Lima's slums. Lima is a beautiful city!" she wrote.

Yes, Lima has pockets of colonial charm, Moorish balconies, exclusive churches, grand dining places, and beautifully kept parks and plazas in some areas, places untouched by ugly settlements of squatters. But seldom, if ever, are the residents of these neighborhoods, be they Peruvians, U. S. citizens, or people of means from other foreign lands, exposed to daily blight. Now and then, an abandoned Indian mother with a handful of tired, ragged, hungry offspring trailing at her skirts (hill women usually wear more than one) will wander along the pretty streets in search of food or a castoff article of clothing. And there are token alms granted to get them out of the neighborhood. We recall early 1962, for example, when political campaigning leading up to the military junta was in full swing, that our Spanish teacher, a winsome Peruvian señorita let us know that she was experiencing pangs of conscience about her pitifully neglected countrymen. Not certain how to ease them, she reasoned that teaching Spanish to Papal Volunteers was a step in the right direction even though our classes were paid for at the going rate. The well-bred teacher was from a family of five, which owned four automobiles. The family's constant worry then was that the downtrodden, under the influence of Communist propaganda, might wrest their every material possession from them if a great saqueo (looting) invasion ever broke loose. Only once in widely separated areas in south Lima was there sporadic, quickly-quelled looting, reported in the daily press as only small uprisings — small potatoes, by U. S. standards.

Lima, as we viewed it, had its serenity marred daily by the potentially explosive social conditions. The miffed woman, so annoyed by our literal impressions of Lima, was a native Limanean who had left Peru with her North American husband a decade before we arrived, but she had maintained her Peruvian citizenship; her family name still commanded attention in some circles of the oligarchy. Though she visited Lima annually, never, she admitted, had she visited the slums.

"I never heard of this Pampa de Comas you write about!" she told us on one of her visits. "Is there really such a place?" She could have discovered the agonizing truth merely by going there to visit the Canadian Oblates or Society of St. James priests. (Officially, Comas is a district now, with its own mayor and some degree of autonomy.) We offered to conduct the Comas tour for her but a full schedule of family business, teas with old friends, and gala dinner parties prevented her from setting aside the two hours needed out of the two months she was in Lima for that visit.

In Lima the little girl (or boy) of the wealthy or rising middle class is chauffeured to every appointment, be it to school, a weekend movie, a trip to the seashore club, a shopping spree along *Jirón Unión*. She leaves a home of exquisite appointments and enters the limousine at the front door and rides along a circular drive behind the high wall which shuts out problems of the street. En route she opens a book and reads. Her limousine deposits her two steps from a fine store, a charming restaurant, an exclusive club. In each place utmost luxury abounds. When she returns home, she steps back into the shelter of her luxurious home, retires for the night surrounded by clean odors, fresh linen, lacy pajamas, the sound of music. Sleep takes her from a veritable wonderland to dreamland.

Later as a society matron, if she still hasn't been jolted out of her dream world, she continues to ignore the squalor, filth, and poverty, the social injustice, the ragged, unschooled masses of her fellow countrymen.

Though some people of means, and those scrambling to achieve such means, still prefer to turn away from the problem, there are growing numbers of Peruvians who do try with utmost sincerity to help. I covered one of Lima's barriadas with a young mother of three whose dedicated help was outstandingly selfless and marvelous, and in God's eyes could only be spiritually bountiful. Her husband was a rising professional man of moderate means; they felt their obligation to their countrymen; they promulgated through active participation Peru's growing Christian Family Movement; most Sundays they attended Mass in a church in a working man's neighborhood, instead of in the select parish in whose boundaries they lived.

To watch Elsa N., a Peruvian lady, lead the way at 7 A.M. through a Surquillo slum in south Lima when many damas of her class were still hours away from their noon rising time was most gratifying while I was collecting facts and pictures for a story. Dogs, which overrun the slums, ran out to pester us. Men leaving for employment or in search of work eyed us suspiciously. What would we want in this God-forsaken place at that early hour or at any hour for that matter? Why the camera? Why the Peruvian dama and the gringo in their slum? You nod to each man, and the peering women, saying "Buenos Dias" and asking how they are — realizing that such a routine question is almost unanswerable when the poor guy has just pulled himself from a makeshift bed, or off the hovel's dirt floor and has shuffled out into a world that offers him so little. Some of them don't answer, just watch, and you can't blame them. Others continue with hope in their poor environment, smiling warmly, wanting to make a good impression. There's no chance to explain to each person that the Peruvian woman and you are going to the new milk and bread distribution center for children and mothers. Once I told a man that and he waved his arms in anger and shouted: "Why are *they* getting all the help? When will something be done for us? Can you open a training school so we can learn trades? Where are these sewing centers we hear about so that we can have one and our woman make clothes for us to ward off winter dampness that's given me my tuberculosis?" In an area where such schools were still only in planning stages these questions were not out of line.

To people in real want, I learned in the slums, tomorrow is too far away.

Only a dozen or so years, really, have passed since the tremendous overflow of sickly, illiterate, and starving people stormed into Lima. Not that those conditions did not exist in once-controllable fashion in generations past. Had the wealthy leaders faced them head on, today's conditions would be minor.

Leaving the barriada after seeing more mouths fed and after

the material for the picture story was complete, Elsa had facts from volunteer mothers about food receipts and distribution. Pungent odors had smacked us in the nose and turned at least my stomach queasy. Very easily the question had come to mind again: "How can you say Lima isn't a beautiful city?" I found myself hoping that the publication of my picture story might help answer the rich lady's question. I left Elsa at the PAVLA regional center and she returned to her own pre-school children. In her own home after she had bathed away the grime, fleas, and possible infectious germs that she had gathered she greeted her children, hoping that she carried nothing that would make them ill in days ahead.

Like a Damien, Señora Elsa N. volunteered to go into the dangerous reaches of her city. Hers was not a trip to Molokai, but her dedication was of the same kind as that of the Flanders priest.

Before considering Lima as the city beautiful, one has first to discover and feel the eternal beauty in the work of those seeking to solve her slum dilemma. Temporal beauty he finds easily in San Isidro's plush neighborhood, the Gran Azul Country Club in Andean foothills "away from it all," in the Plaza de Toros de Acho where the world's top bullfighters come in October, Trece Monedas restaurant, stylish Montericco district and its race track, the private beach clubs. Like the rest, then, we stared, worked our cameras, ate caviar (when visitors from home insisted on picking up the checks), and spent our limited soles on seeing Peru. I'm sure that we were accepted simply as "rich." It would have been nice to have had some distinctive PAVLA insignia that would have caught the eye, say, of two young sightseeing priests approaching us on Lima's downtown main street sometime after we had adopted Lima as our PAVLA home. Those clergymen struck Mary Ellen and me as real lost people that day. Why not help welcome them to our adopted home? We crossed Unión thinking of our first "lost" days on the great street, and, deciding not to let them wander around any longer without guides, we stopped in front of them and said "good afternoon" in English. They were Columban priests from Ireland, enrolled in the Cienegilla language and customs schools conducted by the St. James the Apostle priests organized by Cardinal Cushing. The society was begun originally only with Boston archdiocesan priests but more and more U. S. and foreign priests were joining, and one of them, Father John Moore, of San Diego, was assigned to round up prospects across the land.

"We're looking for a good place to eat," they said and we were off to our favorite Unión eating place.

In those days it was not unusual to hear people say that we were the first Papal Volunteers they had ever met. Most of them inquired about our motives, the money that was in it, the length of time we would work in Peru. So PAVLA public relations work began. One pioneering PV from Bethesda, Md., Robert Clark, once explained PAVLA to his fellow passenger on a train. When they parted several stations down the line, Bob felt he had done a pretty good job of it until the man, shaking hands, said: "Good luck to you and all the People's Volunteers!"

Fathers Louis Dineen and Brendan Sherrard got the PV story, too. Six months earlier Father Dineen was at Northwestern University's Medill school of journalism, brushing up for field work as correspondent for *The Columban Fathers Missions*, the poignant monthly published at St. Columbans, Neb.

On the invitation of Father Dineen, Mary Ellen and I visited *El Montón*, which each of us feels unequivocally is the toughest, most demanding, most thankless, demoralizing mission post of all of those we saw during our work and travels in Peru, Bolivia, or Brazil. In this parish we met Lima's slums at their worst: The surly dispositions of idle men and young boys, the great filth, the moans of the woman dying on a rickety bed with newspapers covering her for warmth and no medical attention. Concerned that we'd never find his Columban parish in the heart of *El Montón,* if we went alone and our personal safety might be in danger, Father Dineen called for us in his little bug of a gas-saving auto. On the way to his people he asked: "How do you get rid of your garbage?"

Immediately, we were to learn that his parishioners live over it, atop Lima's great garbage dump called *El Montón* . . . in Spanish the meaning is "a heap," "a pile" of garbage! Father Dineen said that there were 500,000 tons of garbage upon which some 17,000 people had set up huts of straw matting, scrap cardboard, and tin. Luckier residents had more substantial adobe brick dwellings. But in none were found running water, heat, or electricity.

At a distance, before the stench hits, one sees its warning signs, a thin, smoky haze of smoldering garbage hanging over *El Montón*. Low-hanging clouds drip garua mist upon everything. Kids play in the dirt. Laundry outdoors never looks cleaner than gray. Dogs lying at rest in a doorway only swish tails and flick ears to chase flies but bound to life when someone walks into the area. In winter *El Montón* life is menaced because the constant clouds hold the acrid smoke just above their huts, adding to lung problems.

Five years ago a handful of scavengers built their frugal shacks upon *El Montón,* working the refuse, selling reclaimable materials. First one family moved in, then another and another. The word was out, filtering back to the family's distant hill homes some 500 to 600 miles south and east of Lima. In December of 1963 an estimated 8,000 people, newly-arrived in the capital city from Abancay and Andahuaylas in the Department of Apurimac, crowded into *El Montón* in a week's time, raising its population to 15,000 people, a total which continues to climb.

Standing next to his simple church, Father Dineen told us that the layer of refuse we were standing on was 27 feet thick. The seemingly useless rubbish could be worth $15 a ton or some $7,500,000 when reclaimed and used for fertilizer. He was hopeful that when the tests in progress were completed work would begin to turn the pile into profits.

Six-foot-deep trenches dug along one street for water pipes that never were laid revealed compressed layer upon layer of refuse that had accumulated through the years. Already, because the pipe had not arrived, the trenches were being used for new garbage pits, for outdoor toilets, and for the children's war games.

Of his neighbors, more than a handful we encountered were very good people, some of them expressing gratitude to Father Dineen for something he had done for them in his apostolic rounds. A woman who seemed to be looking right beyond us as she talked, described what she was going to do when she escaped that prison; to us she sounded as if she were leaving that very afternoon. But it would be a long time yet, Father Dineen assured us. There was the man we didn't get too close to because of the rusty revolver he waved in the air. Yet, in passing us on the other side of the dingy street he gave the revolver an extra little wave and in English shouted: "How do you do?"

Bibiana Gomez had lived in this area. We learned that she had died on a bug-ridden bed the week before, after having suffered painful cancerous months in her eight-by-eight-foot hut. Looking up at the hut's pieced-cardboard ceiling, one thanked God it doesn't rain around Lima. Mamá Gomez would have died without the last sacraments had it not been for Oola, just 20, a Swedish convert and member of the Swallows, an organization that sprung into Christian action after Abbé Pierre, the French ragpicker priest, lectured in several Swedish towns. Oola, who had worked in *El Montón* for three and a half years when we visited her neat, simple quarters, had come to ragpicker territory. Fighting a bad cold as she talked, she told how on Saturday nights and Sunday when drunkenness flared up, it was safer for her to stay in the Traperos de Emaus quarters on the big city's south side. Oola had helped to tend Mamá Gomez's needs in her dying days, simple as they were — a change of bandages, a bowl of soup, a decade of the rosary together. Oola also taught reading and writing classes in spare moments, showed mothers how to cook more nutritious meals from their *Caritas* dole, and how to take care of their tiny children — things like using just a little water to keep green mold from growing in their ears.

When Mamá Gomez died, she left behind, Father Dineen told us, three children, a fetid, one-room squatter's hut, and a $150 funeral bill. In her dying moments memories of carefree earlier times returned and Mamá Gomez spoke of them in snatches of mountain poetry she brought from the Andean hills. Perhaps the words were from lullabyes her Indian mother sang to her not too many years before, for this woman had died at the age of 38. Her two wishes at the end were to be returned to her mountain community to die — this could not be, and the wish for a better life for her children — it looked as though this was not to be either. The thirteen-year-old daughter, even before her mother breathed her last, was already living in the same hut with an older *El Montón* man who had taken her for his common-law wife. Knowing this, Mamá Gomez held the thin hope that at least her daughter might be provided for after she was gone. Her youngest son, eight, awaited placement in an overcrowded government children's home; chances were greater that he would be roaming the downtown streets as a homeless, shoeshine boy or possibly he would be taken in by another hill family living on the heap of garbage. The 16-year-old son had already flown from the nest.

Walking amid that king-sized shanty town on a first visit makes one wonder about *El Montón's* future. In stinking odors along dusty, disease-breeding streets of a community that never should be there at all, hopelessness does grip you. You feel it and fight it by recalling some shreds of encouragement. There is Father Dineen and his fellow missioners; then the few doctors who do volunteer work on weekly visits; charitable workers like Oola; British women who dare venture in along with the Jewish women; the Mormons; the Methodists; the Seventh Day Adventists, and others; the sacks of *Caritas* food bringing the only nourishment many of the people receive. And there's the parish where not too many of *El Montón's* people come for services, but where many cluster around for food, medical help, clothing, and advice — some few of them to ask it, others to give it. From 17,000 people the four Sunday Masses were drawing only about 500 faithful when we visited. The Sunday plate collection normally was about 80 soles, somewhere around three U. S. dollars.

We could turn our backs to it and bathe away the clinging grime. But nobody can wash away those *El Montón* memories. We were to return there on C.I.C. assignment and to bring Papal Volunteers fresh from the training schools, explaining that their PV life ahead would have tough moments, but they'd never match those faced daily by the people of *El Montón*.

Among Peruvians, one doctor declared he'd never go there. A general in the *Guardia Civil,* a man who had done outstanding work to improve the social lot of his countrymen and labor conditions for the troops, told us he would not be safe walking in that district in his forest green uniform. *El Montón* has swallowed up hunted felons. A touring midwest priest wilted upon returning from the garbage heap tour, and, sickened for two days following, laid the blame onto something he had eaten. We had been nauseated for sometime after our first visit by the sights and smells alone. Most of the missioners on that beat, unassuming campaigners for the most part, were hard to pin down for a story or picture. Enmeshed in their work as they were, they did not stop to consider with me, an outsider, that the greatest of mission stories was *El Montón,* where if anyone didn't see God in everything occurring during his waking moments there, he didn't belong and *El Montón* would soon have chased him out.

In our rounds of Lima our efforts usually failed to inveigle diocesan representatives to ride with us on one of the ancient streetcars, which Papal Volunteers rode often enough. I wondered then how those tranvias bulging with the press of humanity, could be aptly described at a PAVLA formation meeting back home to people who one day would have to travel in them .

Returning home from work one evening, I found a note from Mary Ellen saying that she might be a little late. "Trying to teach a 9-year-old girl in the corralon how to feed a new baby," the note explained. "Their mother died yesterday." My wife had gone from the clinic to the area behind the wall where the squatters live after she heard about the mother's death. Nobody in that hut knew or cared that she was from distant Kansas; but all sensed the understanding and love being transmitted, as it were, from one to another of God's own, as the work of the Mystical Body was unfolding. This was Papal Volunteer payday.

And there was nine-year-old Lucho, a thin, wide-eyed boy who lay quietly in a bed in our apartment, getting used to the white cast that was setting around the fracture in his left leg. Earlier in the afternoon he had fallen from a parallel bar on the municipal playground next to the parish church. He was taken to Lima's hospital for children. It was so crowded that he was released after the bone had been set and the cast applied and brought to our apartment simply because no one in the clinic knew where he lived — but a bed was needed immediately to allow the cast to set.

"We've got a guest," Mary Ellen told me as I came in the door the day Lucho had been hurt. And she told me about him. "We thought he lived here in Balconcillo but after returning from the hospital he admitted he lives way out in Chorrillos. He only said he lived in the parish so he could keep attending the free afternoon classes."

Sunrise and the boy's father arrived at the apartment together. The man was deeply moved with gratitude because gringos had taken his son into their home, placed him in a clean bed, and Mary Ellen had hurried to him during the night when he called out.

A frown creased the man's forehead as he asked: "And you have done this for complete strangers?"

At that moment another Peruvian learned about Papal Volunteers' apostolic mission work and across Latin America the story would gradually be retold.

CHAPTER VI

PEOPLE ON OUR PAVLA BEAT

"The place matters little if the spirit of fervor
is not there."

— Thomas á Kempis

In *La Prensa's* editorial room a wire editor had just taken us to one
of the two busy teletype machines in a little nook and the very first
item we saw clicking off was the day's Minnesota-Kansas City base-
ball score coming in with other American League scores. It said:
Minnesota, 5, Kansas City 4.

"That's our team!" we said excitedly to newsman Arnoldo Zamora.
"Kansas City!"

"Sorry they lost," the Peruvian offered with the warm, sincere po-
liteness of many Latins. Reporters flitted around the room, checking
Lima street locations on the great wall map, thumbing through dictio-
naries, punishing typewriters, answering telephones, coming and
going on assignment. A photographer threaded fresh film into his
camera. Two girl reporters eyed Mary Ellen's U. S. style clothes. And
really, nobody sat around with his hat on and a "Press" card printed
in Spanish stuck into the band.

Most men in Lima don't wear hats anyway. Indian women from
the hills wearing man-style hats, each distinctively-styled according to
localities, support the hat business in several Latin nations. Derby
hats, which are made to sit squarely on the heads of altiplano Indian
women, are popular around the Lake Titicaca shores bordering Peru
and Bolivia. Years ago, when derbies went out of fashion in the

United States a hustling salesman gathered stacks of them and sailed for South America where to his chagrin he found the mountain men were wearing mostly their colorful knit chullos and provided no ready market. So to the women the salesman said: "Women who wear these hats will be blessed with large and happy families." The derbies went like bed sheets at a January white sale and, when the supply was exhausted, the Indians began producing their own.

Our newspaper office visit was a symbolic Peruvian send-off to PAVLA work. Lay missioner's chores aren't exactly a picnic. Neither, thank God, did our duties prove too overwhelming. As our A's faced up to defeat so too would we fall short of runs at times. But we decided to place our score sheet in the hands of the Official Scorekeeper of All Mankind.

La Prensa became a helpful contact for the Catholic Information Center, which at the time of our visit was still a mere paper project. The newspaper's Sunday feature tabloid carried fine articles on PAVLA and the C.I.C.; one of the articles featuring a half dozen PVs showed Mary Ellen in nurse's white giving an injection to a two-year-old Indian boy while his mother in man-style hat and colorful shawl comforted him. Some mothers paid a token fee for medical services, something like eight or sixteen cents according to their funds. These prices seem absurd by U. S. norms but to an abandoned mother with a handful of children, eight cents buys 2.2 pounds of rice.

It was a year before our arrival in Peru that a study committee of the Catholic Press Association headed by Father Albert J. Nevins, editor of *Maryknoll* magazine, was in the country at the invitation of Archbishop Romolo Carboni. The Papal Nuncio charged the committee with the task of an in-depth study of the nation's mass communications and allied Church attitudes, concentrating on an effective Church mass communications program. Find out, he urged, prevailing attitudes toward the Church on the part of practicing and nominal Catholics. A system of priorities was needed, Archbishop Carboni suggested, for such an immediate and long range communications program.

Two weeks of packed C.P.A. scheduling included interviews with almost fifty high-ranking members of Peru's Church, government, and personnel of radio, press, television, and magazine facilities. Returning home, Father Nevins' committee was joined by experts from *Time* magazine, Columbia Broadcasting System, and public relations firms. Beginning with the Church image and population studies, the committee tackled national health, illiteracy, slum growth, land reform, illegitimacy, poor communications, and custom and cultural traditions centuries old and no longer able to meet the tests of modern times. Social justice pressure bore down heavily on the rich ruling classes and those of the rising classes who were neglecting their brothers in poverty.

The C.P.A. committee fully backed immediate need for a Church information bureau which should (1) be a quality public relations outlet representing the Peruvian hierarchy; (2) prepare Catholic press releases and mass communications programs for secular news media; (3) serve as the secular newsman's contact for authoritative data about the Church and her liturgy, assuring correct, universal treatment of Church articles, information that could not possibly become conflicting or twisted in the nation's outlets.

Lima had more daily newspapers than any U. S. metropolitan center. Eight different newspaper "empires" competed for advertising and circulation when we were there. Two, possibly three, were credible journalistic heavyweights with the balance tapering off into sheets varying from good journalism to quite poor imitations of it. Lima editions spoke out freely on passing issues and the two leaders, *La Prensa* and *El Comercio,* hammered back and forth at each other with the regularity of the Horace Greeleys and James Gordon Bennetts of our nation's penny press of the 1830's.

In the decision in 1961 as to where Mary Ellen and I would be assigned in Latin America my background in mass communications dictated Lima as the location, although we had lightly thought about Brazil, possibly somewhere along the Amazon river. As for Mary Ellen, PAVLA program advisers assured us that nurses were in demand everywhere, so our course was to Incaland as the first married PAVLA couple from the Diocese of Wichita and the second from Kansas.

In the Catholic Information Center we learned that presenting the proper image of the Church (a dynamic and apostolic Church working to implement religious and social teachings of Christ among all men, as the fact-finding committee emphasized) was a herculean, almost thankless task, though the top metropolitan dailies were quite cooperative. But, when an obscure, hand-set, mountain or jungle weekly filtered back to our C.I.C. office and we saw the articles containing our credit line, to a man we experienced warm feelings of accomplishment from the C.I.C. director, Rev. Joseph F. Michenfelder, M.M., through the four-man staff.

Our office, for example, updated accomplishments of the people in the "City of God." On Christmas Eve, 1954, several thousand Peruvians, who had been displaced from high Andes' villages lacking life's basic needs — food, health, work — poured from their slums in Lima and Callao and marched en masse ten miles just outside the metropolis' southern limits. By dawn they had stepped out their little sandy tracts, setting up another ramshackle, estera (straw matting) hut community. The Peruvian press was credited with naming it *Ciudad de Dios,* City of God. Accompanying the marchers was a statue, Our Lady of Mercy, mounted on a platform carried by men at the head of the march.

The Mother of God has henceforth held her revered place among City of God character residents. Every Christmas Eve since 1954 they have re-enacted the original procession in the now-sprawling community that today tries with noticeable success to unshackle itself from barriada conditions. Many small government-sponsored block homes replace the original straw quarters, and water and electricity are available for those who can afford them. Otherwise, people walk blocks to fill water containers, and use kerosene lamps for lighting.

In the summer of 1961 clusters of *Ciudad de Dios* people, carrying pots, buckets, pails, and glass jugs, waited in line for their daily water supply from a faucet extending from the outside wall of one of the buildings of the Maryknoll Fathers in their Child Jesus parish. Other people, not in need of water, dressed in their "best" were also arriving. A police band showed up. Many of those milling around the water supply couldn't read — if they could have afforded a newspaper

—the accounts of the imminent arrival of someone held in world-wide esteem.

Richard Cardinal Cushing, pastor of the Archdiocese of Boston Catholics and revered friend of many non-Catholics, appeared soon among the water carriers and thousands of others — poor, middle class and wealthy alike — that day. So did Lima's Archbishop (now Cardinal) Landazuri and the Papal Nuncio, Archbishop Carboni. Displaying his broad grin and chipping off bits of the Cushing wit, His Eminence delivered a message of hope that was translated immediately into Spanish. He promised to build a church for the City of God.

Funds came from the north; Maryknollers started the building project. Father William R. McCarthy became pastor. Initially, Mary Ellen expected to be assigned there to help set up and assist in the new parish clinic, and Father McCarthy fretted in advance about her prospective assignment wondering how he'd ever get through to his parishoners that this Mrs. McCarthy was not his wife. (At the time in Lima there were eight McCarthys in religious and lay mission work, none of us related or previously acquainted.) An obstacle arose, however, and Mary Ellen was assigned to an in-town clinic.

On C.I.C. assignment one damp afternoon I arrived at City of God with camera and note pad, hoping that the terrible overcast would roll out as fast and unexpectedly as it had rolled in from the sea. While circling the church under construction, snapping views here and there, I was approached by three little girls dressed in white school smocks already showing the week's wear. I had just used up the last of my film. In Peru children in public schools attend Saturday morning classes for a five and a half day school week. Extra long noon siestas compensate for the extended week.

The youngsters took me in at a glance. "Take our picture?" they asked.

"Sorry, niñas, I can't. No film left." They watched as I removed the roll, sealed it, and dropped it into the gadget bag. Sometimes you can get by with an empty camera, snapping dozens of "pictures." Kids get such a bang out of posing, most of them never expecting to see you again or the snapshots.

"Are you from a newspaper?"

"No. The Catholic Information Center in Lima."

"What's that?"

"We write stories and take pictures about the Church and social justice. Newspapers use them."

"Where do you live?"

"In Balconcillo. What grades are you in at school?"

The older two were in fourth and second. The tiniest girl, tightly and shyly clutching her sister's hand, didn't answer but her sister said *transición,* which for them is in between kindergarten and first grade.

"This will be a pretty church," I said.

"Much better than the community hall," the eldest girl replied.

"Do you girls go to Mass on Sunday now?"

"Sí . . . every week."

Looking down at them, you hoped that in twenty years they would not be wandering aimlessly, husbandless, worrying about food and clothing for the ragged innocents tagging at their heels.

The fourth grader was walking at my left while we crossed the sandy soil toward the parish rectory; my gadget bag over the left shoulder was held close to me, to prevent it from bumping the little girl's shoulder as it had moments earlier. To my right the smallest girl, just next to me, held tightly to her sister's hand. Looking down at her, I asked: "What's your name? Carmen? Dora? Yolanda?"

The other girls wouldn't help her; after a momentary pause I heard her say: "Liliana," looking up fleetingly at me as she did. Her glance then darted back to the sand at her bare feet, in her inexpensive orange-colored plastic sandals.

"What a beautiful name . . . Liliana!" Now I caught a new trace of a smile from her. Suddenly she took hold of my right hand. The sensation was startling.

Was this shy little Liliana? She was tall enough to reach my belt line, small enough to own one of those tiny voices that most times make an adult bend down closer to hear all that is being said. Beneath her half-opened white smock she wore a baggy, almost buttonless sweater over a dress soiled enough . . . all evidences of deplorable conditions causing many children to go to school that way . . . concerned not over what they wear but rather that they are actually able to go to school!

Liliana clutched my hand now as well as her sister's in new security. Her grasp was firm and warm. I, a stranger out of nowhere, had for the briefest of moments entered her world. Her pensive looks, a word now and then, I was hypnotized by her while we walked . . . Liliana and a gringo Papal Volunteer. Such shreds of happiness, and then she gave my hand a tender, childlike squeeze. Here was another child looking for just a little kindness. I returned Liliana's affectionate little squeeze, ever so lightly, and her dark eyes danced, though she could not know how I was torn apart within myself at the thought of her deprivation.

These thoughts and others rolled around in my head as I wondered, too, what sort of public reaction would have resulted had I dared to walk with these little girls in Mississippi, for example, where at the moment in 1962 the segregation stand and battle against James Meredith entering the University of Mississippi were shaming the U. S. image in world headlines. You would have wondered about it, too, for God put little, innocent Liliana on this earth as a Negro.

The three girls skipped off down another dusty street leading to school as I neared the rectory where Father James Madden, assistant pastor those days in Child Jesus parish, was hurrying out.

"Come on along," he called out and I trotted over to catch up to him. As he zipped up his black jacket to ward off the dampness, he told me about a woman who had come to the parish social center and told about a man who had been lying in a street nearby for two days. He was still alive, she had said, but mighty sick. Turning the corner several blocks from the rectory, we saw him ahead in the dirt road street, an occasional battered car driving around him. Curious youngsters held their distance. He was lying on his back mumbling unintelligible words. Someone had sheltered the man somewhat by placing a cardboard box over his head with an opening in one end at the neck. One side of the box was torn away. Several *pancitos,* little bread rolls, now dry, were stuffed under the opening of his tattered herringbone tweed coat.

"I'll have to get a taxi to take him to the hospital," Father Madden said. "We'll never get an ambulance out here." Then giving a quick thought to other things, Father Jim asked, "Did you get some good pictures?"

"Hope so," I replied, reaching out and pretending to gather in a handful of garua mist so bad for outdoor pictures.

The next week's C.I.C. news packet to Peru's beat carried a couple of views of the church under construction; copies went to Catholic Press Association outlets in the U. S. But the star of that story in my notebook was Liliana, whose picture I could not take.

Two and a half months after Mary Ellen had begun daily trips to the clinic of Our Lady of Guadalupe parish, Father Garrity (with three underworked nurses in his clinic and one teacher short on his overworked school faculty) asked if she would consider teaching one of the lower grades. A nun-teacher had become ill and doctors advised her to return to the states, he explained. Mary Ellen had never taught a day of school in her life, but she was in Latin America to help where needed, preferring to continue in her own profession, of course. She asked to be given one of the kindergarten sections so that the nun handling that section might take the higher grade.

One Friday evening she returned from the clinic loaded with books to assist her in the new role of kindergarten teacher. "Sister wants me to come to school tomorrow and she'll fill me in on some class work for a starter," she told me.

"When do you start?"

"Monday."

As the second semester of the Peruvian school year began on August 13, 1962, ending the two weeks' vacation over late July Peruvian Independence Day holidays, Señora McCarthy looked out across a classroom of some 60 boys and girls and said: "Buenos dias, niños!"

In the apartment that night she said: "Did you notice in the Mass of the two martyrs this morning that one of them was St. Cassian? In A.D. 258 he was stabbed to death by pupils using stilettos in his school!"

No, I hadn't noticed it and I recall we didn't discuss it any more, but during the next eighteen months I did notice her love for those children grow; and, when on her birthday she remained at home with a cold, some sixty little notes arrived, each one wishing her "Happy Birthday," the phrase printed out in English. Papal Volunteer Paxton, who delivered the greetings (and who filled in as "baby sitter" for her that day as he called it), insisted he had nothing to do with the letters. Her "emergency" teaching, aided by the sisters and Mrs. Isabel Salazar, teacher in the other kindergarten section, was to carry over into another year, for when that initial semester ended Sister Marie Agatha asked if she would continue teaching. Mary Ellen agreed but asked that it be just half days because she wanted to set up a school health program in the book storage room and work there afternoons.

In previous years, when the new school year began, physical examinations were given by doctors who charged for their services. Checking the roster of school parents in her newly opened health room, Mary Ellen learned that a number of fathers in that growing, low-medium income neighborhood were physicians and dentists. "Why not get the parents more involved in their school?" she asked Father Garrity. "Couldn't we ask each of them to volunteer an hour of their time for these examinations? Mothers could give time helping to fill out examination forms." Several of the doctors made it a point later to thank those involved in the volunteer examination program for inviting them to contribute to their children's school progress. People to people effort is moving beyond its gradual beginnings; Latins are searching for ways to help their Latin America. Seven years after Guadalupe school opened, the first cost-free immunization shots were arranged through the district office of the National Ministry of Health. Again, pupils benefited by a PAVLA-initiated project that got Peruvians successfully involved.

Morning teaching and afternoon health clinic work occupied my wife through the 1963 school year. My C.I.C. work continued until January of 1964 when full-time work was assigned from Chicago PAVLA headquarters to locate and operate with Mary Ellen the first PAVLA regional center on South America's west coast; for this purpose we rented a house large enough to accommodate twenty-four adults.

Because we joined PAVLA with the complete understanding that monetary gains would be placed aside for at least three years, we were distressed when occasionally some Peruvians and now and then a gringo showed their disbelief that the PAVLA program appealed to the layman's apostolic values, rather than to any desire for material gain.

"You wouldn't come down here to work like this for almost nothing in wages," some said. "In the United States everyone is rich, with big houses, cars, and lots of money. Why give that up to come down here?"

Most Peruvians, it must be said, did understand that lay people could come to their land with such motives. But there was always the fellow who insisted that we must have some financial "angle." Like the Peruvian man of some wealth whom we met in Father Dan McLellan's credit union office one day. He invited the priests to come out to his hacienda any weekend for hunting and then looked my way and somewhere between the padres and the laico (me) the offer ceased. No point in proving to him that the seat of my trousers was just as shiny as those of any mission padre.

Most children, too, had an idea at an early age that we from the United States were walking mints. Name the parish in Latin America that didn't have an annual bazaar as a fund raiser and you were naming a debt-free parish where reliance upon such means was no longer urgent. It's safe to bet that every parish started by North American or other foreign missioners had the annual kermesse as many were still paying plant debts. PVs strolling among the many booths would be smothered by people selling raffle tickets on food baskets, plaster of Paris dolls, bottles of wine, or baby chicks. Tattered kids from the corralons swarmed around you, pulling at your clothes: "Could I have a sol to try my fortune on the food baskets? Can I have that pan you just won to take home to my mother?" Watching the little boy trot off carrying the pan you gave him, you shook off such cynical thoughts as: "Will his mother ever see that pan? Will he sell it at the market down the street and dart back with a few soles to play on the hamster race? Does he even have a home? How many of his buddies is he going to tell about you, so that in five minutes you'll be beset by more youthful pleas? Suppose that kid was abandoned by his mother years ago after his father ran out on her?" Shaking off those suspicious thoughts, you thought instead of the kid slipping into his straw shack and handing the pan to his mother, who gratefully stroked his matted hair.

To such kermesses Mary Ellen and I normally carried 100 soles each, about $3.75; about twenty soles were set aside for ourselves because an afternoon bazaar did things to the appetite. Chinese foods were inviting, so were the Peruvian anticuchos. What was more tasty than a tamale when the sun was trying to return to Lima on the first Sunday in October? You peeled back the tamale's corn shuck wrapper and were careful to eat around the harmless-looking but red-hot native peppers.

Gradually, Latin Americans turning to the Church with renewed devotion are realizing that kermesses alone are not enough, nor are raffles of TV sets or refrigerators, to support the church, school, convent, rectory, health clinic, playground, and other parish projects. But the lesson of giving justly to Church needs is their problem, too, as it is in the U. S. A. PVs *can* help the natives understand that our overabundance of material things is achieved largely because we work very hard to have such goods in the U. S. A.

On June 3, 1963, amid worldwide mourning over the death of Pope John XXIII, Papal Volunteers in Balconcillo were subject of a scandalous report. The previous night police had raided a neighborhood apartment to halt traffic of a cocaine peddler, and had confiscated some sixty pounds of coca leaf. Rumor had it that the raid was on the North Americans instead of on the apartment building next door. That's how we made our money, people said, why we complained about a water shortage — we used too much in processing narcotics! Our apartments were in fact too often without water. But tell the PV, when he was lathered from head to foot after youth work on the parish playground — and the shower supply quit — that he was using the water in the dope traffic!

Later, the PV was among volunteers at the parish clinic when 700,000 persons in Lima received smallpox vaccinations in the Minister of Health's crusade. For three days people streamed through vaccination lines with the Guadalupe clinic getting its steady share of the grand total. In our parish two PVs and several youth club members registered them, presenting pink slips which entitled them to public assistance. Mary Ellen was with the nurses in the vaccination lines and on my Saturday C.I.C. offday a couple PVs and I washed hundreds of upper arms with alcohol and cotton balls. As they streamed down the line who should appear but the woman, followed by several of her children, whose tongue had wagged most freely about PVs pushing narcotics. No doubt she had forgotten, or wanted to forget the whole nasty thing, for when she came in the line for her arm scrubbing her smile was big and broad. Priests serving as parish assistants, nuns from the convents, Peruvian youth from clubs patterned after C.Y.O. groups collaborated in the massive national program, described by *La Prensa* as without precedent, to prevent a possible smallpox epidemic from sweeping the nation.

Some of the slum dwellers, of course, like their shiftless counterparts on welfare roles in the United States, kept their hands out and as long as alms kept coming they would never busy themselves with a gainful job.

On the other hand, there was Alfonso Tapia, father of nine children, steady worker, and fine example of the faithful family man in a nation where too many men abandon their families. Like tens of thousands of others, Alfonso came to overcrowded Lima from northern Peru looking for that Utopia that had lured others.

From a wretched slum environment Alfonso Tapia, after several years of hard work as an auto body repairman and welder, removed his family to a better dwelling atop the flat roof of a complex of Balconcillo business houses. Gone were the congestion and the stench, and for Mrs. Tapia there was even running water. In this simple, private rooftop surrounding the Tapias made their way, faithful to their religion. Alfonso, in his early forties, busied himself daily with auto repair, and to supplement the family income his wife took in laundry which she did by hand. When I took a picture of her hanging clothes on the line, she told me it was the second time in her life that she had had her picture taken, the first when she and Alfonso posed eighteen years before in their rented wedding clothes. A mangle washing machine was delivered to the Tapias, a gift of the Catholic Youth Organization of Wichita's Church of the Magdalen, paid for with money earned when members served a pancake breakfast after Sunday Masses. The machine, of course, made life easier for Mrs. Tapia, and brighter on wash day, which for her was every day. I remember that she couldn't realize that the machine was a gift with no strings attached, so she returned to the parish and wanted to hear Father Garrity reassure her again that the washer was truly theirs, a gift from U. S. friends.

Little Maria Tapia received her first Holy Communion on December 8, 1963; the feast of the Immaculate Conception is traditionally the day for Peruvian first communicants. I saw Mr. Tapia walking from the crowded church after he had craned his neck to see Maria receive the Host for the first time; his thick black hair was slicked down, his only suit clean and pressed. He went off to work and was never to be with his family again. As dusk came over the city that evening, the vehicle he was returning after a repair job ran out of gas along Argentina avenue on the way to Callao. While he was pouring gasoline into the tank at the side of the road, a pickup truck, according to witnesses, rammed into the back of the car, pinning Mr. Tapia in the wreck. The truck driver backed away from the fatally injured man and damaged car and sped off into the gathering darkness. Two days after Christmas, Mr. Tapia died in a Lima hospital. People in the United States, touched by the troubles of the Tapias, sent enough money to pay the family's rent ($12.50 per month) for a year plus some extra funds for current bills.

Papal Volunteers serve not only in their assignments, but they become vital liaison agents between home and mission welfare projects. When visitors arrived from the United States, or anywhere for that matter, we made extra effort to be PAVLA informers. We visited one evening with a group of 25 tourists from Kansas City, Kansas, in the elegant Gran Hotel Bolivar. Mary Ellen was dressed in her Sunday best of gloves, earrings, perfume, hat and all the "accessories." One of the visitors from Kansas exclaimed when he saw her:

"But I thought missionary women wore plain dresses, big thick glasses, severe hairdos, and would be home reading the Bible at this time of night!"

To the Kansan and anyone else in earshot she replied:

"We're twentieth-century missioners. Mission work isn't all clinics, scabby kids, remote jungles, or slums. Missioners are needed just as much here in the cities among the growing middle class as they are among the poverty-stricken. Here we lead three lives beginning our day with Mass and the suggested spiritual exercises. That's our incentive; it's not the $70 a month."

As the Kansan, as well as I, listened attentively, I found myself learning some new things from my wife.

"There's our work in the clinics," she said, "youth centers, the classrooms, social service outlets — things like that which are our second life. Occasionally, for our third life we put on Sunday clothes and get a chance to meet you people. And these contacts are just as important as our work with the Peruvians."

Surrounded the following day by so many thousands in want in Lima's barriadas, one of the touring Kansas women had tears in her eyes as she remarked: "We've heard about those conditions, but you have to see them." Too few of the tourists see such conditions; only a few care to when invited. And when they do, and understand the needs, results are often rewarding, like the arrival of the sewing machine given to Pampa de Comas slums earmarked for delivery to Virginia Jackson, Boston nurse at her PAVLA post with Our Lady of Peace parish there. Months before, she had mentioned to touring Milwaukeeans Hazel Cavey and Agnes Anderson that a couple of sewing machines for her mothers' classes would mean the start of cooperative clothing production for markets nearby after family needs were relieved. Reams of correspondence were exchanged with a company in the states, Miss Cavey, and the company's Lima field branch. After much perseverance, the sewing machine became a reality in one of the parish community center rooms.

But you have to close your eyes to red tape, push on, and sometimes to close your eyes is to dream or to try to dream.

Six hundred and thirty miles from our Lima quarters I was not dreaming when on a PAVLA news-photo jaunt I lay sleepless on a very hot, humid night in an Arequipa hotel room. In the middle of the night somebody stopped outside my door and opened it. Shafts of hall light cut across my bed as I sat up. "You're in the wrong room, caballero!" I bellowed. Begging my pardon, he departed as I padded over from the bed, rechecked the door lock, and then braced a chair under the knob for good measure. Might be asleep next time the guy loses his directions.

Not five minutes later, I heard a scuffle outside my door, a man's muted voice and a woman's, calling for help. How much of a hero is a foreigner supposed to be under the circumstances? Had I dashed into the hallway I might have found a distraught girl or woman, and there I'd be standing on the scene as other doors flew open. I waited in my room and considered the possibility that the gent who had barged into the room earlier might have cooked up some little game with a friend to involve me. I chose not to play the hero's role; almost as suddenly as the scuffle began, it stopped. Before the multi-colored macaw began its racket at daylight and stretched its plumage in the garden below, I was fast asleep. I remember the young girl and her child or little brother who sometime before had come to the apartment below the convent. She said a man on a motor scooter was annoying her. Could she have a ride to her home nearby? A priest visiting us at the time advised us not to get involved with his car so I walked her to her home a few blocks away. A bona fide problem that time. But you can't count on them all.

Later that morning at the Arequipa airport I met PAVLA Field Representative Kevin Dwyer on the incoming plane for the continuing Satco Airlines hop to Juliaca, a village perched some 12,500 feet in the Andes valley near Puno; our subsequent PAVLA travels took us into Bolivia. There on a cold winter night in July we visited St. James the Apostle priests in Oruro before returning to our lodging with the Canadian Oblates where Dwyer checked out new Papal Volunteer requests. We were seated close to the fire when in walked a priest wearing a beret and dark jacket over his white habit. He was introduced to us as Father Terence, a Dominican from Chicago. I dug into my memory. "Father Terence," I said. "But what did we call you back on the Marquette campus — Al Holachek?" And that we did. Now our paths crossed anew in Bolivia. The Dominican priest who had worked with university students in Cochabamba, Bolivia, for several years had come up to Oruro for similar duty and was staying with the St. James group at the time. We saw each other about 20 years before in Milwaukee!

Returning to Lima aboard the plane from La Paz, I was busied with thoughts of stories to be written, photos to process, the little Arequipa incident, and the wonderful reunion in Oruro. I was distracted by the man in the seat next to me who politely told the steward that his coffee, just served, was cold. The steward wondered, saying it had been brought steaming from the galley! My fellow passenger, having mentioned earlier that he was a South African professional mountain climber returning from adding two new Bolivian peaks to his list, plunged his right index finger down through the black coffee to the bottom of the full cup and held it there! He looked up at the steward and smiled. The second cup, really steaming, arrived. And there was no test this time. Successful mountain climbers take no needless risks. Nor do matadors in the bullring, nor presidential candidates facing a broiling Latin American mob, nor bus drivers leaping clear of their vehicles when university students toss a Molotov cocktail. Brave men, some of them. Brave men. And you look at them and wonder.

CHAPTER VII

WHO ARE THE LATINS' BRAVEST MEN?

"Muy macho!"

Very manly . . . very manly!

What more does this muy macho compulsion mean to the Latin American male in day-to-day living, whether he's lord of a lavish hacienda, master of a gracious urban mansion, owner of a modest, mortgage-free, low-middle class stucco home painted blue, tenant in a rented efficiency apartment, or a neglected soul in an estera straw slum shack?

How does machismo affect daily life cutting across his professional, religious, family, political, or recreational ethics?

To most Latin males, machismo for centuries has meant POWER. The ideal muy macho male is the Walter Mitty mixture of Adonis, Simón Bolívar, Henry VIII, Paul Bunyan, Sir Walter Raleigh, Belmonte, and Hemingway. The eat-drink-and-be-merry muy macho male's yen, his joy when accomplished, is to scoff the Casper Milquetoast type out of the plaza, to deride the pastoral work of El Padre in the parish.

No United States President since Franklin Delano Roosevelt captivated hearts in Latin America as did John F. Kennedy. When in 1961 President Kennedy, bricklayer's trowel in hand and vivacious Jacqueline speaking Spanish at his side, dedicated Bogotá, Colombia's massive Ciudad Techo housing project of the Alliance for Progress built for rising low-middle income classes, newspaper editors used the phrase muy macho to describe JFK in their midst.

But the JFK manliness was different. It meant living his religion faithfully, concern for the oppressed, and a world at peace amid a family-oriented society in brotherhood, regardless of race or religion. His successful demand in 1962 that the Soviets remove their missiles from Cuban bases sent many Latin American caballeros into spasms of envious delight. Fewer Castro-type beards were sported. The Cuban dictator lost face considerably and his machismo rating took a nose-dive. Most Peruvians vigorously hailed their military junta's order to dispatch two Peruvian warships to assist free nations in the Caribbean blockade of Cuba. To all Peruvians, including the Communistic National Liberation Front which reluctantly recognized the fact, Mr. Kennedy was the heroic victor in the showdown to *desprestigiar* Mr. Khrushchev, to lessen his prestige in the eyes of the world.

In Latin American cities plazas are incomplete if not adorned with impressive statues of muy macho men, from the very first of them down through the ranks of men who shaped a proud national heritage in battle, in statesmanship, science, philanthropy, the arts, personal sacrifice, and only occasionally in religion.

Pizarro the warrior, weighted down in armor, charges on his horse a block west of the Cathedral in Lima, off Plaza de Armas. General San Martin is astride his mount in the central plaza named for him. From a Jesus Maria bus window so often on my way home from work I watched and waited as traffic stalled at Plaza Bolognesi. Six major thoroughfares poured a tangle of honking vehicles into the circular drive around the plaza. Caught in the tangle, carbon monoxide about to do us under, I watched muy macho tempers skyrocket in the streets. High above it all, grasping the flag of Peru in his left hand, a pistol in his right, Francisco Bolognesi (famed Peruvian general who informed invading Chileans in 1880: "We have sacred duties to fulfill and will fight to the last bullet.") looked down upon us all. Often I thought that a twentieth-century Lima motorist, plucked from those caught in rush-hour plaza traffic jams, ought to be done in bronze and placed on a pedestal as one of the nation's bravest.

Another candidate for honors might have been the policeman standing smack in the center of this busy intersection with his white helmet, white gloves, forest green uniform with trouser cuffs tucked into black, shiny boots bravely blowing his whistle.

What about the matador with cape and sword in the Plaza de Acho ring as El Toro charges? For my moments of truth, however, I wouldn't put him on the plaza monument . . . unless . . . maybe Manolete. For the others . . . a hall of fame in some matador's museum. (There's the obvious and inevitable bullring custom of setting aside distant, top row seats in the sun for the poor aficionados who queue up hours ahead for those least desirable seats at negligible prices. Aristocrats seated in the shade pay very high prices to watch star matadors like "El Viti," "Murillo," "Litri," or "El Cordobés" from Europe in the grand October fair of Peruvian bullfighting. Thus is the gate price averaged out for the campesino or the shoe factory stitcher to enter for a song — "ole" from a distance, and bake in the sun.) Brave men.

And I think of street vendors selling muffins, apples, sweets, combs, or razor blades from their little stands along the sidewalks during uncertain times as when bank workers strike, when taxi drivers gang around the palace with their protest signs, when professional university students stir up discontent and riots in turbulent plaza meetings. (When Khrushchev was in the public eye, they wanted his name submitted for the Nobel Peace prize.) Those vendors press close, risking tear gas, risking rochabus water dousings, taking the risk of having their little stands knocked down in the stampede when police or Guardia Civil troops arrive. Such vendors, male and female, seeking a meager livelihood, rightfully earn a place with the brave ones.

There's the hard-core Aprista political backer walking along one evening when thousands of opposing Odristas are assembled in a grand rally preceding presidential elections. Elbowing his way into the outside ring of the crowd, he shouts: "Viva Haya de la Torre!" Supporters of Odria turn on him pronto and next morning from his hospital bed the APRA man tells reporters how he got clobbered.

The sun rises and sets on soccer as Latin America's great participation and spectator sport and even after the sun has set you can still hear scuffling of shoes on street pavement "fields" near a lamp post. (Such commotion during troublesome times causes a person to look twice to determine if the clatter comes from a lively soccer game or people in flight.) Soccer referees in Latin America vie for badges of bravery, but they're not plaza hero timber.

So, then, who among Peru's and Latin America's men are the bravest?

Once a week, sometimes oftener, you see them. Though they're not out in great numbers, their ranks are increasing — Latins who attend Mass every Sunday as their Catholic religion requires. In a culture hypnotized by machismo tens upon tens of thousands of Latin males consider regular church participation degrading to their image in the home, neighborhood, shop, office, classroom, marketplace, country club . . . yes, even sitting in the plaza out of work. The idea of going to church regularly isn't popular with the Latin male.

Native Latin American priests, and there are some wonderfully dedicated, Christ-inspired men in their ranks, have had to buck this anti-spirituality since colonial times. This is not to say that colonial Catholicism had an absolutely impossible struggle to gain ground, nor is it to reflect on today's sincere, practicing Latin Catholics. But colonial Catholicism did have some peculiar quirks about it. Years ago a Spanish official in charge of one federal Peruvian department with all the haughtiness of his pre-independence position instructed his private chaplain to alter the standard Hail Mary prayer for the exclusive use of his family. The prayer was made to read:

". . . Holy Mary, mother of God, *our cousin,* pray for us sinners . . ."

Historically, they wear their religion on their sleeve however neglectful they are of it. From colonial days to the present the muy macho male has been organizing to defend himself, not too concerned about the Ten Commandments or the Seven Sacraments. He harbors resentment toward the social, economic, and religious structures surrounding him.

Speaking during a Papal Volunteer Day of Recollection, Father Carlos Alvarez Calderon, trained at Louvain and Lyons and today one of Peru's most dynamic and inspiring sons of the cloth, told us:

"The real national sickness in Peru is not the *"verruga."* It is the inferiority complex."

Because theirs is a history of oppression, which will be briefly re-

young Peruvian girl is a voluntary teacher in Pampa Comas. Roofless, the mat walls of her "classroom" aid vacy, concentration . . . Adobe block desks and chairs used in slum school in *barriada* on south edge of mbote . . . Maryknoll Father Thomas Garrity has plete attention of Lima girls eager to listen and m, and eager for identity . . . Gradually, "colonial a" adobe architecture disappears. Large downtown dings like 22-story Ministry of Education building appearing.

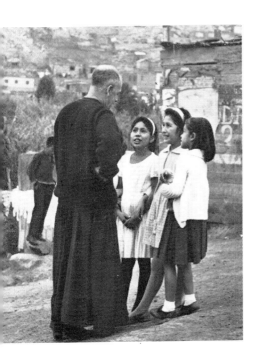

North American religious and
aiding Peruvian clinics and ho
attend a medical conference in
. . . New hope for Latin A■
Young men gainfully employed
ing cinder blocks for schools,
centers, and homes in Lima's
. . . Papal Volunteers visit with
Peruvian patients and friends
long clinic hours begin . . . Ma
classroom — hopefully tempor
amid ageless dedication in Ch■
slums.

Two Peruvian women learn hospital charting from Bette Foote (right) in Sicuani where PAVLA nurses help staff government hospital . . . Lima's downtown La Merced church depicts churrigueresque facade, a feature of many colonial Latin American churches . . . Peruvian pastor, serving workers near Chimbote, raises fighting cocks to supplement meager income. Such fights are legal in Peru . . . Puno area Maryknoll priests instruct catechists in evening classes after tiring day's work. In unheated rooms fingers turn cold to chalk, books, pencils.

Rented quarters (above) for the PAVLA Regio[nal]
Center in Lima housed as many as 25 voluntee[rs,]
PVs in Peru, Ecuador, Bolivia, and Chile u[sed]
these facilities . . . Richard Cardinal Cush[ing]
celebrated Mass in the center and visited with [them]
during breakfast . . . Time out for PAVLA rec[re]-
ation. Volunteers with Peruvian friends and ai[des]
watch assualt on *piñata* during Halloween c[os]-
tume party.

counted here, Peruvians are quite susceptible to an inferiority complex. When the ancient, pre-Colombian cultures of Nazca, Chimú, Chavín, and Tiahuanaco people vanished, Inca chiefs ruled with iron fist until the 1530's when Spaniards invaded.

After independence was gained in 1821, foreign clergymen were expelled but oppression in no wise vanished from the Peruvian scene. A small, exclusive body of Creole families controlled the government, fashioning laws favoring their oligarchical ways, buttering the bread of the landed gentry. The impoverished were given only token consideration. They were subjected to a rubber-stamp formula of suppression until only a score of years ago. Political power factions jockeyed for national control and eleven presidents were deposed in the 1826–1908 period. One died in civil war and two were shot. From 1821 to 1962, some half a hundred leaders or political groups ruled the nation. Countless political parties were born as people rallied around a candidate; if he won, the party lived; if he lost, he and his party disappeared. Stability in Peruvian politics has increased steadily since five presidents ruled the nation during an 11-day period in 1931, one rapidly succeeding the other. After 1932 when a new president, General Sanchez Cerro, was assassinated because of an undeclared border war with Colombia over the Amazon river village of Leticia, the violent political struggle leveled off but has never disappeared. Politics still flares up into military junta rule, the most recent occurring in July, 1962, when Peru's military-controlled government was established and was to last for a year and 10 days.

From past disturbances many Peruvians salvage some notion of personal prestige in clamoring for individual power. A Bolivian once told us this is responsible for selfishness being the main drawback of the Latin. Mixed with the inferiority complex — or a part of it — is skepticism which causes some to seek evasion of issues through drink, chewing Coca, women, or a supermanish, lively, mass interest in soccer or in the more daring bullring.

The Peruvian who considers first his duty to God and then his place among men is the Peruvian promoting operation "New Start" for the Church's and nation's re-establishment. As in any other nation, there are citizens elbowing their way up for material gain.

One Peruvian told us that ruling families of the nation felt their inferiority complex showing when they looked across borders and continents to observe more progressive living among their foreign contemporaries. Within the nation the middle-class man makes it clear he is above his rising low-middle class countryman; the latter ranks are growing to recognizable proportions — the important class without which Latin America could collapse. Low income group citizens, embittered by memories of being ignored by the upper classes, raise their hands little to help the poor, illiterate campesino, believing themselves above that too-long neglected class. Downtrodden slum areas are overrun by dogs, many, many dogs . . . which people retain despite the need to feed them at times when their own larder is bare. These are protection for their masters' meager possessions. Finally, the poor Indian, with no human class beneath him, has no recourse, when the mood hits him, but to kick the dogs.

Indeed, Father Alvarez Calderon reminded us, North Americans should never forget that Peruvians have a cultural heritage which they seek with aggressive dignity to preserve; yet, "If Peruvians are told that they are progressive, religious, wonderful people, they will cheer and applaud. But they won't believe it. Whereas, if you tell the Germans, for example, that they are progressive, religious, wonderful people, they won't cheer but they will believe it."

Because for so many generations a social justice consciousness was not encouraged by the oligarchy, Father Carlos, his priest-brother, Father Jorge, Peruvian and foreign religious and laity have only in the past decade made their beginnings toward this goal, introducing, so to speak, Christian foundations to be demonstrated in the marketplace. The muy macho urge of the Latin male has been their major block, a block only gradually being nudged to the side.

Dinner was at 9 o'clock the night we visited the home of a retired medical officer of Peru's armed services. The meal was special-occasion Creole, featuring roast duck stuffed with rice, boiled yellow potatoes (one of Peru's fifty varieties) garnished with a cheese and hot chili sauce, boiled egg slices, and black olives. There was a side dish of cebiche, fresh fish pickled in lemon juice and seasoned with raw onions. The meal was a real delight. The colonel, his wife, four of their children, Mary Ellen, and I were seated at the table amid Peruvian dinner hour *ambiente* atmosphere of sheer enjoyment. The colonel's mannerly solicitude extended from the refilling of plates all around to certainty that no word of conversation was missed because of the Spanish; if so, he'd quickly switch to English.

Alone in another room later the colonel and I looked at a display of firearms behind the glass-enclosed wall rack. It was then I asked how many children he had.

"Bueno," he began, using the standard one-word <u>introduction</u> to answer much as we use "well" in our conversations. "My wife and I have six children, four of whom you met tonight. But I have eight children . . . if you know what I mean." Now the colonel unwrapped his machismo complex for whatever it might accomplish to impress this North American guest in his home. He wanted me to know that somewhere, because of his ability to finance the arrangement, he had his casa chica hidden away where another woman attended to more of his offspring. But his braggadocio boomeranged, spoiling the remainder of an otherwise pleasant evening. To make an unpleasant situation worse, it was Mothers' Day, a special day in the hearts of Peruvians, too.

The colonel typifies the Latin male whom Father Vincent T. Mallon, a Maryknoller reassigned last year from Peru to open his community's first mission in Venezuela, described in this manner: "Many Latin American men see no conflict between their ceremonial notion of religion and their personal way of life, which may include taking a mistress, missing Mass every Sunday, sharp business transactions, and underpaying workers. But in most cases when the arteries begin to harden, he makes his peace with God."

Continuing his observations, which were backed by almost a decade of priestly work both in the cosmopolitan cities and remote altiplano Indian villages of Latin America, he said:

"It is easier for a Latin American to be a Catholic than not to be one. In the first place he is inevitably baptized a Catholic as an infant, or at least as a child. Most of the better schools are run by the Church. Weddings, funerals, and dedications are almost always Catholic affairs. Patriotic celebrations, inaugurations of new presidents,

and school commencements are usually presided over by the local
Apostolic Nuncio or Cardinal.

"Political leaders are expected to take part in great annual religious
processions as on Good Friday or the feast of a patron saint. But too
often his religious practice is the result of social, economic, and political pressure, rather than the result of personal conviction, particularly
before late middle age," Father Mallon said.

Hope for the entire Latin American structure lies in the increase
of more Christian families. When Father Mallon spoke, he very
assuredly felt within him the grief that such truths bring to the
spiritually-heroic Peruvian, the Christian Family male who is no less
a man in his home, his work, and free time endeavors. The Maryknoller in Venezuela could supply a growing list of such men
emerging bravely from a pitiful history of international machismo,
men guiding their children toward this new Christian concept, setting
good example in their neighborhood, difficult as it may be for them.
And Father Carlos can point to his increasing number of young male
contacts on campus or at their places of employment who belong to
this rising group giving the lie to machismo.

In the parish of Our Lady of Guadalupe in Lima, the quiet, diligent
work of Maryknoll priests, first to arrange cursillos (short courses in
Christianity) and then to follow up with Christian Family Movement and Legion of Mary activities, has resulted in a nucleus of
parish-centered families. Among such Peruvians we had the pleasure
of meeting at least thirty couples formed into three CFM discussion
groups.

Our first contact with one of those CFM fathers — his Sunday
Mass assignment was helping to pass collection baskets — led to our
pleasant introduction to the Gonzales family. During the offertory of
the 8 o'clock Mass at Guadalupe parish a United States $1 bill, con-
spicuous among clinking bronze sol coins flipping into the wicker
basket, alerted him to the arrival of more North Americans. He
spotted the U. S. bill, since it is slightly larger than the Peruvian
five soles green note which drops infrequently into his basket. Passing the collection basket that Sunday was Rigoberto Gonzales, who
with his pleasant wife, Sara, has two sons, Carlos and Luis, and two

daughters, Maria del Carmen and Ana Maria. Rigoberto was born in the high Andes valley called the Switzerland of Peru, in the town of Caráz, 294 miles north-northeast of Lima. From Caráz' Plaza can be seen the stately, twin-peaked Huandoy mountain, towering just to the north of Huascarán, Peru's highest at 22,205 feet. (Huascarán's north glacier edge cracked loose on January 10, 1962, just eighteen days before we left Kansas, sending down an avalanche that buried 3,500 Peruvians.)

When tragedy struck the Rio Santa Valley that day, Rigoberto was already a transplanted Limanean, having taken work as a public school teacher. The growing family lived in a crowded apartment just at the edge of the park and Guadalupe parish, their spiritual and material life making forward strides. Rigoberto, as one of the parish's first cursillistas, saved and planned to begin his new block home with an attached garage for the car he hopes one day to buy. Before we left Lima, we visited them in their new home — not yet completed — but their answer to those who would rather continue pursuit of machismo, bogging themselves down, and holding the nation down with them. Next to his family devotion Señor Gonzales is devoted to his teaching, which is at the elementary level. Not long after making the family's acquaintance, however, we realized that he was applying religion to his family's formation, and that religion also accompanied him into the classroom.

To illustrate Father Mallon's earlier reference to the Latin's ceremonial notion of religion, there is no greater example in Lima — and the cult is spreading across the nation — than the annual *Señor de los Milagros* (Lord of the Miracles) procession, held October 18, 19, and 28th. During this religious event the muy macho man is perhaps closest to mixing his faith with his masculinity. Today's procession dates back three hundred years when a Negro artist named Benita adorned the wall of a small Pachacamilla chapel with its Calvary mural. A devastating earthquake four years later leveled the city and three walls of the chapel, leaving intact the wall containing the Calvary scene. To colonial Peruvians and Spaniards this was omen enough; they started devotions centering around the mural. In 1760 the first public procession took place, the occasion calling for eight men to carry the first anda platform bearing the picture. In the past 200 years the October procession has grown so that annual devotion of Peruvians seeking protection of our Lord from damaging earthquakes attracts as many as 250,000 people to the route over which the painting is carried. The popular Brotherhood of Our Lord of the Miracles, with its list of men waiting to join, provides eighteen teams of one hundred men each to carry the silver and gold laden platform and replica now weighing slightly more than two tons. Forty-two men carry the cumbersome platform, putting their shoulders under the four-by-four timbers on which it rests and march in step to the slow beat of funeral music. One team will carry it about one hundred yards and at the sound of a gong will set it upon the pavement where another team takes over. At the city hall, the president's palace, and the cathedral bordering on Plaza de Armas, they tip the great anda in salute to the mayor, the president, and Cardinal Archbishop of Lima as 60,000 people — mostly garbed in the penitential purple habit of the October cult — slowly crowd into the plaza. There is hymn singing mixed with the shouting of people separated from friends in the great crush. The Brotherhood is muy macho then . . . straining, sweating, eager to be among the elite of Peru's men allowed to carry the anda. For this public honor they pay a $10 annual donation, and in accordance with the Brotherhood's rules, usually go to Confession and receive Communion during October, so the Church in Peru has extended the Easter Duty deadline to October 31st. During the first of the three public processions, the Brotherhood carries the platform for approximately seventeen hours from the Church of the Nazarene to Our Lady of Victories in Lima's eastern La Victoria district. The following day the procession returns to the Church of the Nazarene just off Avenida Tacna over a longer route, one that requires twenty hours to cover. A smaller downtown procession is held on October 28th.

Some Peruvian men have told us that too much of the annual event is for show only. We know Peruvians who never participate. One, a newsman asked me: "Where are so many of them the rest of the year . . . at Sunday Mass, helping to support their pastors, living proper family lives without mistresses?"

Indeed, though more women than men are seen in the huge crowds, they are not permitted to assist the Brotherhood. One sees mothers holding sick children above the crowd so the child can see the passing mural. They call out: "Save her, Lord! Save her, Lord!" Poor and rich alike mingle in the throngs. One newspaper even published a picture of two well-known pickpockets who had arrived in Lima from Argentina. The caption read, "to assist in the festivity of Our Lord of Miracles and slowly rob the faithful of their wallets." Muy macho hombres they were, done in by alert members of the nation's plain clothes detective force, the PIP, *La Policia de Investigaciones del Perú.*

One PIP officer working with the division of aliens is Alberto Mariaca who lives with his wife and children in Father Garrity's parish. Alberto is a high-type Peruvian, the Christian Family Movement type. He was chosen from among his fellow PIP officers to attend a course of training at the FBI school in Washington, D. C. One of his family's proudest possessions is a photograph published in *La Prensa,* showing Alberto receiving a handshake, diploma, and warm congratulations from J. Edgar Hoover.

The Maryknoll Fathers, the Columban Fathers, the St. James the Apostle Society, the Norbertines, the Chicago Carmelites, the Jesuits, the Canadian Oblates of Mary Immaculate, and the growing list of parishes have an increasing number of families whose fathers qualify for the new breed of Peru's bravest — men saying "no" to machismo and sticking to their principles.

CHAPTER VIII

LOS YANQUIS IN INCALAND

Contrary to some beliefs, "Yankee Go Home" or "Fuera Los Yanquis" signs in Latin America are rather rare. We did see some from time to time in Lima and in the hills, but when the time arrived for me to satisfy an urge to photograph such signs I used up a Saturday afternoon traveling on foot and in buses in search of my subjects. Along Avenida General Arenales someone had splashed the hurried message in black paint on a high, canary-yellow wall bordering massive Employees Hospital, just off the Manuel del Pino corner. Chances are the sign isn't there today. If a new coat of paint hasn't already covered the wall, then other slogans such as "Lower the Bus Fares," "Land or Death," or "F.L.N. Meeting May 1 — San Martin Plaza, 7 P.M.," most likely have crowded out the original sign by now.

No reflection is meant here on the neighborhood where the anti-Yankee sign appeared in the Lince district. Rejects from decent society roam the city and countryside of Peru just as unwashed, bearded malcontents with straggly hair gather in U. S. cities and, wherever they congregate, leave their calling cards.

As expected, however, the sign I photographed had the shaky initials "J.C." following the "Yanki Go Home" slogan. There was no space on the wall for the letter "P" which normally is included in the "J.C.P." and which stands for the Young Peruvian Communists. Members are not a clear and present danger to national unity and freedom; but they must not be dismissed lightly either, because of some in the ranks who are passionately dedicated to Cuba, Moscow, or Peking. And, plagued by international communism's perpetual headache, they wrangle among themselves over where their allegiance is fastened. Many J.C.P. hangers-on are confused youth running with the pack, looking for identity. They wouldn't know if the Communist Manifesto was written by Marx and Engels or Ernest Hemingway, and in time their commie loyalty wears thin. The dedicated J.C.P. members, however, are keen and perceptive and, should Red rule ever take over, they could be in vital positions in the banks and transit unions, or in politics as members of the Senate or Chamber of Deputies. Those boys do not do the painting of illegal wall slogans; they persuade José and Maria to do the dirty work, to be the ones caught with brushes in hand and to pay the fines or serve the jail terms.

Thirty-five months in Peru brought Mary Ellen and me into many situations wherein we visited with, observed from a distance, or flatly ignored some of the Yankees we encountered. It must be said that there were many North Americans who made us proud to be fellow citizens. These latter certainly were not responsible in the mind of the Latin journalist when he wrote:

"Too many travelers head south of the border expecting everything just like it is at home but a bit more picturesque. When it isn't, they complain. They criticize, they compare . . . loudly! This is no way to win friends for yourself or for your country. We'd like to suggest this as a motto: 'May every Mexican you meet consider you the nicest foreigner he has ever known.' "

Sadly, some Yankees overseas deserve such criticism; we had this in mind in a downtown Lima hotel lobby when Mary Ellen and I awaited our Catholic Relief Service friend just in from Ecuador. The cosmopolitan atmosphere bustled with an interesting concentration of people. Travelers rushing to and from airport taxis, people moving in and out in tour group clusters, businessmen arriving for luncheon appointments — Japanese, Peruvians, Yankees, and others among them.

Not twenty feet from us was THE Man From THE United States standing with a handful of compatriots and two Peruvians. THE Man From THE United States was talking, and our attention was drawn immediately to his conversation because after hearing Spanish almost constantly in public English comes through like a clap of thunder; and, it was the first time in Peru such continual use of profanity was heard by us, coming across the lobby in the traveler's loud voice. "I couldn't get the — babe to share half the hotel rent with me. . . ." Laughingly, he told his group about the airline hostess he bothered 30,000 feet in the sky; and now he was ripping into the morning side trip just completed, a break from their Lima business conference. The trip took them to famed Pachacamac Inca ruins, eighteen miles south of Lima across the coastal desert countryside on the ribbon of the Southern Pan American asphalt highway. "They dragged me out so — early and rushed us out to this — place, nothing but a — big pile of clay and the — price they asked!" He was continuing to sell his nation down the river as our CRS friend joined us and we left the hotel.

Pachacamac is the adobe ruins of what was the most flourishing and important city on the west coast of South America when the Spaniards arrived in the early 1530's. Dedicated to Pachacamac, the Inca god of fertility, the temple was constructed of baked bricks in A.D. 1350 and commemorated a victorious march by Pachacutec from Cuzco to the sea. Legend says that there stood the oracle when the Inca Viracocha prophesied that white men would appear, bringing about the fall of the Inca Empire. The fact that rain is infrequent has helped preserve the adobe remains. Standing at the topmost parapets of the once glorious fortress and temple, with cooling Humboldt Current breezes blowing in off the Pacific, the surf breaking and sending up its timed roars, with only the sun and sky above and Lurin valley's green growth to the south and east, a person could close his eyes and imagine Incas pouring out of the sand hills on pilgrimage to their shrine. Nature has been good and saved the historic place, but the man from the United States, while at Pachacamac, was unable to see the beauty. He was too busy damning everything about him.

Not condescendingly, I used to call Pachacamac the poor man's Machu Picchu, which is the more famous early day Inca citadel located on a mountain top near Cuzco, 725 miles southeast of Lima. People short of time and funds look upon Pachacamac and return home to say they have seen some of the Inca culture. Today, engineers and chemists are trying to find the secrets of the Incas' construction and of their colorful dyes. Visitors to Pachacamac couldn't have seen as many pure stock descendants of the Incas: women carrying their wares to quaint mountain market plazas wearing rich-colored shawls, or village mayors strutting with their silver-studded canes and conch shell horns — people and artifacts right out of the Inca period.

Some of the tourists would ask how many U. S. citizens were living and working in Peru. That total was revealed to us February 13, 1963, in the dining room of the Crillon hotel at a dinner reception of the American Society of Peru in honor of U. S. Ambassador and Mrs. J. Wesley Jones, newly-arrived after five years' duty with the State Department in Libya. (The dynamic American Society of Peru has been active since 1917 and counted some 650 members as of July 4, 1963.) Of those Americans few know that Peru's standard gauge railroad, the world's highest reaching 15,806 feet above sea level after departing Lima and chugging into the Central Andes mountains, is the construction of Henry Meiggs, who after building Fisherman's Wharf in San Francisco, lived in Peru during the years 1870–1893 and supervised its building. The railroad goes through 68 tunnels, crosses 55 bridges and zig-zags along 22 switch-backs where the sheer mountains refused to be conquered any other way. In 1928 Elmer Faucett, newly-arrived from the U. S. A., launched Peru's first domestic airline which is still operating.

Peru had close to 8,000 U. S. citizens living within her boundaries when we were there; some 4,000 U. S. passport holders are on Peru's economic scene, people employed by the U. S. automotive industry, pharmaceutical firms, oil and fishing industries, the mines, and even in orchid production in the jungles. The remaining four thousand are with the State Department, church organizations, Peace Corps, private business or artistic endeavors, and wives or husbands of Peruvian citizens.

As their Peruvian days unfolded for the Joneses, Mrs. Jones soon scheduled an afternoon a week at the City of God slum clinic. There, sometimes aided by one or another of their daughters, she did volunteer work for the Maryknoll priests and sisters and worked with

PAVLA nurse Ethel Knecht. And there was Dr. Gordon Rock, of Davenport, Iowa, who arrived for personal medical work in the central Andes. He and his college-age son bunked with us overnight at the Lima regional center, and told us of their plans to work five weeks in Peru. The Iowa obstetrician-gynecologist was to persevere but three weeks; however, he returned home saying "it was the most frustrating experience in my life." In the mountain town of Sicuani he found himself working with very little equipment, no x-ray, no laboratory facilities, and very few of the basic medicines. "Everywhere I turned I found so many things to do and no possible way of doing them," he said. "It will take a concerted effort on the part of North Americans to supply necessary equipment and money. I strongly feel that other doctors should go to Peru. They can begin to see things which hamper the Peruvian doctor and then start to help him and his patients. It must be through a process of understanding by both groups. That's why the work being done by the Sisters of Mercy and PAVLA workers is so important. They are the ones who are really laying the foundation for the work to come. The difference between the volunteers and me basically is this: Their main job was to save souls, my job was to save lives. I simply couldn't get by without the proper tools and medicines."

PAVLA people, of course, and the religious too, learn that much work with the Latins has to be done first with the bodies; only then can the apostolic work succeed.

Because of the large U. S. colony in Peru, on July 4, 1963, *La Prensa* published a twelve-page special supplement paying homage to the United States. Editors explained that if *La Prensa* had existed that day in 1776 when the U. S. broke formally with the British, the front page would have carried an eight-column banner headline about it. Washington and Jefferson got good play in pictures and there was a four-column story filed by *La Prensa's* "Correspondent in Rome" in which the Vatican's reactions on the new U. S. independence were noted. A couple dozen U. S. companies operating in Peru were generous with their advertising in this supplement.

Along the Peruvian news beat our first year I rushed one day toward the U. S. Embassy, amid swarms of people hurrying to their jobs, to wrap up business with the U. S. Information Service office. I found the embassy gates locked. Two Peruvian Civil Guards with automatic weapons slung across their backs patrolled the sidewalk next to the high fence. Two U. S. Marine guards could be seen inside near the telephone switchboard station in the stately, four-story building; that closed-down situation reminded me: It was the Fourth of July!

Having suffered the ordeal of getting downtown in the bus, I felt that there was no point in going back home at once. Leaving Avenida Wilson for España, I walked the long block, turning left at the Palace of Justice where Paseo de La Republica cuts across. Aging tranvias swayed to and from the heart of the city, kids hanging on the backs for their free and dangerous rides. In bronze on the green lawns stood haughty llamas and near them the campesino wearing his colorful mountaineer chullo knit cap standing between two oxen, symbols of rural life in the high sierra. Often I wondered if the statue of the bronze man and his oxen didn't bring back memories to the illiterate campesino when he trudged past perhaps suffering from tuberculosis, out of work and hungry. Life in the mountains is difficult but for the hill dweller removed to Lima's slums it is worse. In the mountains there is sunshine instead of the long winter overcast; there is a clear water stream easily available in the mountains, no crowding in line at the corner spigots; there is a leisurely tempo of life in contrast to the frenzied one of the city.

Across from the Palace of Justice, Peru's in-town penitentiary for men, built at the start of our Civil War, was being razed to make room for an impressive civic center. Beyond the penitentiary property, just across the wide *paseo,* is a building shaped like New York's Flat Iron building; here Great Britain maintained her consulate and chancellory offices, my new goal for that morning.

The elevator doors slid shut and the very British receptionist smiled pleasantly after being told that I was from the C.I.C. and the U. S. A. The warm reception on that damp Fourth of July lifted my spirits. I was among the British because our newly-emerging C.I.C. had launched a pleasant working rapport with Mr. Arturo Dyer, second secretary, who immediately asked to be called "Pat."

And the fact that he knew and loved the Irish ditty, "All Praise to St. Patrick," was one of the delights of our days in Peru, nurturing an interesting camaraderie in our inter-office liaison that on occasion touched upon a fleeting aspect of our social life — but first, this preliminary explanation.

On the night of our first Peruvian Easter Mary Ellen and I were Father Garrity's guests in fashionable Club 91, an Italian restaurant atop a tall building along Avenida Wilson, an excellent place to view for the first time the lights of Lima at night. Dining out was a respite from studies for us and a change of pace for Father Garrity, whose extra-parochial duties for Cardinal Landazuri and Archbishop Carboni often took him into blighted areas, unseen now from atop Club 91 because, without electricity, the slums were blacked out of the panoramic view. The traditional Easter baked ham was excellent. On the way home we stopped for a visit with a North American family whose breadwinner was employed by a New York firm doing business in Peru. Later, driving to the pensión, we explained to Father Garrity why we'd rather not begin socializing with other U. S. married couples in Lima living on high overseas salaries. In due time, where we lived for six months with only three of everything for the table — three plates, three knives, spoons, and forks, and three straight chairs — it was to be more clearly understood why it would be impossible for Mary Ellen, as a housewife, to return dinner invitations, and the like. On PAVLA stipends this was out of the question. Single Papal Volunteers could more readily accept these gracious invitations; living in shared apartments, it was not likely that the men, for example, could invite a U. S. couple over for a home-cooked meal. We decided with Father Garrity that there would be other ways to dialogue with U. S. married Catholics in Peru about the new trends of lay missionaries and what they had to offer in Church aggiornamento. Everything went fine for several months until the workaday contact with the British people crossed over rather enjoyably into the social one. In September we were invited to a cocktail party at the Dyers.

Half a hundred people arrived that night to fill the Dyers' cozy basement party rooms on the high bluffs where picture windows looked out upon the Pacific Ocean along Miraflores' malecon drive. The evening provided new contacts for our information center work and an opportunity to talk about PAVLA. Because some members of the diplomatic corps and their wives were present, newspaper reporters came. Flash bulbs popped! In *La Prensa* the next morning one photo showed the Dyers' daughter in a discussion with us, glasses in hand. No matter that we tried to put across to the reporter about our PAVLA work, Mary Ellen's clinic duties, the C.I.C., such facts did not appear in the story, but our names were spelled correctly.

By and large, the Peruvian press, exclusive of sensational sheets, did well in evaluating U. S. news events, giving them front-page coverage if merited. When John Glenn orbited the earth three times in February of 1962 and Chubby Checker "twisted" his way around Latin America in the autumn of that year, there was good play on both stories. The James Meredith violence at the University of Mississippi also received notice. Photos showed Meredith escorted under guard to classes. The death of the French newsman at Oxford was carried front-page, in a five-column headline. Past troubles in the U. S., recalled now, merely demonstrate how domestic problems are problems, too, for U. S. citizens off in foreign lands where news media pounce quickly on them. Some Peruvians asked us why we come to Peru to help lessen misery when in our own land racial strife is one of the most troublesome problems. The question is not easy to answer.

Upon occasion, Yankees in Incaland enter marriage with Peruvian citizens and because of the many Catholic baptisms in the nation the required civil weddings must be followed by the sacramental wedding. After one such civil wedding between a Peruvian and a U. S. citizen the happy couple signed the registry of the mayor, kissed, and looked forward ecstatically to the church wedding. But already several of the North American guests were congratulating the young "wife." Behind us stood a North American priest, an acquaintance of the couple, who exclaimed: "She's no more a wife than I am until she gets him down to the church for the wedding."

Behind the priest there gathered a little group of North Americans, mostly salesmen. While one was complaining because his $70 Italian-made shoes were not satisfactory, another, a woman, was telling how wonderful it was to be in Peru again. "We tried it back home again in South Dakota for awhile, but it was just too much after being here as long as we've been. No maids, you know, on Ed's U. S. salary and that was a lot of getting used to again. We could not get used to it, so we're back."

Let it be explained here that in Peru most Papal Volunteers did have domestic help. While preparing to leave for Latin America, we heard a program director get very annoyed about PV girls in Lima having a maid. Certainly a maid creates a normal impression of extravagance for PVs, but when one learns firsthand the facts of the nation's economy, pay scales, and unemployment problems, the "champagne taste" impressions disappear. Domestic help, male and female, has just about the bottom rung on the Peruvian or Latin American income ladder. Men in the street-sweeping gangs are worse off because they don't get meals on the job. But for many displaced mountain men and women without education or money when they arrive in the large city, the opportunity to become a muchacha (girl employed in the kitchen and home) or a muchacho (male domestic counterpart) is a godsend. At least they have a roof over their heads and a better than even chance to eat, even though the household servant's calling is one of the most exploited and patronized south of the border. For people living on U. S. industry or state department salaries, to have one, two, maybe three domestics working in a home or garden is not out of line and would be the norm.

We were without a muchacha for six months while living at the convent and it took some scrambling to do our own housekeeping with only one day off a week. Later in the Balconcillo apartment after a month or so without one and when our income was supplemented with aid from the C.I.C. office and occasional article sales, we felt that having a muchacha was in line, and our first one was quartered in the small room for that purpose on the flat roof of our apartment. She was on duty only until we learned that her brother was bringing his laundry for her to wash each week. With her went her complaints to Mary Ellen how tired her arms were each week when it was time to do *our* laundry. Another girl was with us until her

storic Peruvian art, in black ceramic,
ancient Chimu civilization pre-dat-
ncas . . . children from Our Lady
adalupe parish, in Lima, cuddle rag
sent by pupils of St. Patrick's
l, Walnut, Kansas . . . Roses for
favorite statue, two mountain girls
outside Sicuani cathedral at Easter-
. . Rockslides make lofty Andean
perilous. Passengers in a "truck-
alight and walk across danger zones
river edges vehicle over "rough"
along route.

Haughty Andes llamas are used for cargo as well as meat and hides at La Oroya, 120 miles east of Lima at 12,000-foot elevation . . . Young couple, expressive, hopeful, arrives in mountain town of Sicuani to arrange church wedding . . . Valuable hours are lost in the mountains by healthy men who could be busy if industry were available for their willing hands.

regular weekly free time unofficially included extra days off, extra nights out. Experiences with domestics did help us understand the situation. Our last muchacha was that second one, a nineteen-year-old girl who every day took three hours of afternoon classroom instructions with the second and third graders at the nearby Mary-knoll school. She had never attended school during her mountain days northeast of Lima, an area where the pre-Inca Chavin culture flourished, some anthropologists hold, from as early as 1000 B.C. to the time of the Incas.

Other Papal Volunteers assisted muchachas in spiritual and personal growth, sending them to catechism classes, helping them prepare for first Holy Communion, straightening out marital tangles, seeing them gain needed weight, seeing them buy their first new sweater or plain dress from their initial incomes. Without the work as domestics these wandering, penniless ones from the hills might have followed the desperation courses into houses of prostitution either government-sanctioned or operating clandestinely in the sprawling cities. Extravagant as it would seem back home, the idea of a muchacha in a PAVLA dwelling is seldom that at all. Three years pass all too fast as it is; time saved by the PV from household chores is time gained for PAVLA extension outside the home.

There was little difficulty distinguishing between the two types of North Americans we met there — the haves and the have nots. But there was one unpretentious young man over and above both types whom we met at a stylish Miraflores wedding reception. Rodman Rockefeller, son of New York's governor, was in Peru on business. Young Rockefeller wasn't complaining about $70 shoes. Rather, he explained some of his business in Latin America. Venezuela has attracted Governor Rockefeller and family for years. Also the New York politician's son wanted to know about Papal Volunteers for this was his first contact with them. He was given the program's aims, Latin America's needs, facts about the shortage of priests, conditions limiting opportunities to advance more local men successfully through seminary training to ordination. From his six foot plus height he looked right at you through his plastic-rimmed glasses; Rodman Rockefeller wanted to know, wanted to find out, and you felt the man's sincerity. Finally, he excused himself, and went off to join several builders of small homes around Lima for credit union members of Father Dan McLellan's internationally renowned social justice programs which have been featured in many U. S. and Latin publications.

One hundred and one other U. S. men I came upon, all wearing the Air Force blue, had a common, off-duty goal to do their part in getting Peru's "Boystown" on its feet. Though the men didn't seek publicity, they made good C.I.C. material distributed to Peruvian and U. S. mass media outlets. The counterpart of Boystown, U. S. A., is City of Boys, Peru, fifteen miles south of Lima just off the Pan American highway. Neglected boys have been coming there since 1955 when an Italian Capuchin, Padre Iluminato, set aside parish work in the Lima suburb of Chorillos to help homeless and wayward boys find better lives. Borrowing ten small tents for a period of ten days and with twenty abandoned slum boys about him, he left Lima and the group pitched their tents on a patch of desert. By the time the borrowed tents had to be returned, the boys had completed the bare shells of two adobe brick bungalows on the sands. And *Ciudad de Niños* has been expanding ever since with more than 200 boys now sheltered there. The main, two-story white building against the backdrop of high sandhills looks like an isolated Foreign Legion outpost on the sands of the Sahara. Nearby is the temporary chapel dedicated to the Immaculate Conception. When I saw it three years ago, it had only the barest of necessities — a very simple altar, a handful of ancient pews gratefully accepted as castoffs from a Lima parish by Padre Iluminato and Padre Rodolfo, a fellow Capuchin. But there was that homeless boy kneeling ahead of me on the bare floor, saying "Hail Mary" in a half whisper.

Here, on their first work day the American airmen arrived with $200 worth of brooms, mops, pails, cleansers, and brushes for a real "GI" scrubdown party; those supplies remained at the base after the party was over; on regular visits the airmen saw that they were put to routine use. These Americans, men of an aerial photo-mapping team from Albany, Ga., arrived in November of 1961 to photograph Peru's coast, mountains, and jungles, work now aiding highway and resource development in a nation where nature has kept many products from market. In spare hours, these volunteer airmen were missioners themselves, teaching the boys how to keep their buildings clean, getting up soccer games, teaching them to play baseball, and bringing them some shreds of love that the boys hadn't ever had. A GI barber spent his free time cutting hair. Scenes of their work were filmed and as a result of their showing at Air Force bases in Panama and the U. S., increased aid arrived as military chaplains encouraged troops and their families to participate. U. S. airmen stationed at Peru's Las Palmas airfield chipped in a dollar a payday so that some $100 monthly helped Padre Iluminato's growing project. Water was a constant problem until troops in Lima and the Panama base paid for half the plastic pipe needed to bring in drinking water. In many ways men in U. S. armed services serve not only their nation but help reduce neglect among mankind in every area they visit. Growing numbers of college students, too — and we worked with them from the Universities of Michigan, Notre Dame, and St. Francis College of Brooklyn — spent summer vacations on the slum scene. We found them at Boystown. All their efforts were expended out of the range of television cameras.

Many Yankee tourists see Cuzco. While taxiing in from the high sierra airport, however, guides fail to point out the tumble-down compound of buildings where behind walls other Yankees operate a catechetical school for illiterate Indians brought in from remote villages. There in the compound, Sons of Mary Brothers continue the successful work that Maryknoll Father Thomas Verhoven began in 1961. The community brings in seventy Indian students at a time for the training courses. Learning their catechism, they return to their people with the first knowledge of God's work, word, and love for them. The staff at the school had graduated more than 1,500 students at the time of our C.I.C. interview and the total grew to 2,400 in early 1966. Graduates occasionally return to the brothers with accounts of intimidation; Communist leaders in some villages have chased them out, threatening harm to them if they return.

From the PAVLA family in Lima several returned home to enter religious life after completion of their three years. One, whose parents had been converted from Mormonism, is LaRae Dudley of Jensen, Utah, one of the first PVs in Latin America. Following graduate work on a Los Angeles campus after PAVLA, she entered the Graymoor community of Franciscan Sisters of Atonement in Garrison, N. Y. Sister Ellen Theodore, the former Sally Hanlon, of Needham, Mass., returned to South America as a Maryknoll sister.

I remember hearing the Peruvian aristocrat flatly state: "Educate a chollo (mountain Indian) and you have another thief or revolutionary." I parted with him in disagreement. Some of the Latins would rather that the gringos get out and not upset their selfish system that is beginning to crumble. At times there were negative feelings for the Yanquis, as when Washington reduced the sugar quota for Peruvian growers in 1962. At such times the Papal Volunteer is better off sticking to missionary problems, so when I passed the plump woman selling magazines at the downtown stand and she asked me if I was from U. S. A., on the spur of the moment I offered a mental reservation, saying I was from Germany. She didn't ask East or West. And I stuck the news magazine in my pocket and walked off wishing there wouldn't be so many bus fumes hanging low in the street on the misty day.

CHAPTER IX

THE CHURCH'S AWAKENING

"Priest! . . ." he called after us in English, then repeated his cry, "Priest!"

Father Michenfelder and I were walking from the parking lot toward a new workday at the Catholic Information Center. Glancing back, we saw him leaning against the high wall that closed off the lot from the street. A hatless, gray-haired man of about sixty, he motioned to the Maryknoll missioner who began retracing his steps.

"See you in the office," I said, walking on ahead.

Priests know that people at times feel a need to go to confession "right now" and might stop a confessor anywhere. Was this such a time? I wondered. Maybe the man was a beggar. From his blunt tone, he may have had an axe to grind. But priests can wield axes, too. I recalled the U. S. priest walking toward the mountain train in the Sicuani station when a couple youths shouted that he should go back to the United States, he wasn't needed in Peru. The priest grabbed one of them by the shirt front, pinned him against the wall and said: "Will you go to the seminary and study to take my place so I can go back?"

The youths apologized — harmless boys just seeing how far they could go, then backing down and respecting the person who called their bluff.

Religion follows a bumpy road in its current Latin American buildup. The incident of the man calling out to Father Michenfelder that day remains clear in my mind because of the tone in which he

105

called "Priest!" It seemed a surface clue to some aching pains within. Actually, the man wanted money, nothing more. And meeting him later I learned that he still wanted money as he offered for a fee to give me a tour of Lima's cathedral, telling me that he had learned a little English in San Diego, Calif., while working there years ago. *Priest* was one of the words he remembered from World War II times.

Surrounded by the two extremes of Latin American life — great wealth and great poverty — the Church seeks to regain her rightful image, and this will be achieved only through better understanding when more of her illiterate people are educated, when those now scorning her begin to respect her publicly. Needed is an area of gray between the obvious black and white that now exist. And until that time, strong faith is essential for those foreigners hoping to assist the Church in reaching her goal. And equally strong faith is called for in Latins now loyal to the Church, people who are embarrassed when their countrymen belittle the Church.

The taxi driver said: "Sí! I'm a Communist! But the minute the Communists attack the Catholic church I'm finished with them and will fight for Padre José!" The bus passenger strongly criticizes "the solid gold pillars they have in the big churches downtown. Out here (and he pointed to slums seen on the drive into the city from Jorge Chavez International Airport north of Lima) that gold could be used for the poor people." I asked if he went to Mass on Sundays and if he helped with his sol or two contribution. "I don't go to church much and I have nothing. The rich should do it," he replied, an echo of the common idea that the Church is only for the wealthy!

Aware of this image, the Church is trying hard to change so that all will recognize that it is for all those who believe in God. This truth gradually is being carried along trails in the mountains and jungles and on the city streets.

In a little shop near Lima's general post office at the approach of the new year the rush is on for large full-color calendars featuring St. Martin de Porres, St. Rose of Lima, St. Michael the Archangel, and a collection of assorted art — brave bulls taunted by the cape, dancing Quechuan Indians, mountain scenes, and Pacific ocean marlin fishing off Cabo Blanco (Hemingway was there, caught one, and was miffed when moviedom didn't use it in "The Old Man and the Sea," using instead a fake marlin.) Also, posed, undraped women of U. S. or European nationalities are among the stacks of calendar art. In many business places and restaurants in Peru one sees the Sacred Heart, Blessed Mother, St. Rose of Lima, or other religious art prominently displayed with most likely a small, electric vigil lamp below glowing reddish soft and eye catching. Occasionally, a lighted candle flickers. And after a while one gets over the shock of seeing on the very same wall, right next to the religious art, calendar pictures of nude or scantily clad women. This is part of the Latin's way, an age-old pattern.

On paper, Peru has one priest for every 5,800 Catholics, ranking her third, after Brazil and Venezuela, in the continent's shortage of priests. Clergy involved in teaching assignments or administrative posts, or restricted to contemplative monasteries, or otherwise withdrawn from parish work, make it more realistic to set the figure at one priest for every 12,000 Catholics in Peru. Ireland has a priest for every 450 Catholics; the United States, one for every 680 Catholics; and Italy, one for every 950 Catholics. Brazil, the largest Catholic nation in the world with 70 million Catholics, has a priest for every 6,400 Catholics.

His squeaky shoes during a PAVLA retreat at Villa Maria in Chaclacayo focused attention upon a deacon from Lima's San Toribio archdiocesan major seminary, Oswaldo Guerrero, who was making a private retreat preliminary to his ordination. The chapel stillness was broken only by tinkling of altar bells and the squeak of Oswaldo's shoes as we filed to the communion rail. God bless Oswaldo! More squeaky shoes on dedicated men are needed in Peru and Latin America. A week later in San Toribio's chapel we heard those same squeaky shoes approach the sanctuary for the ceremonies of ordination. Oswaldo was the only priest ordained that year. Three other seminarians were advanced to deacon or subdeacon. During our Peruvian work about fifteen priests were ordained annually, the majority of them being religious — Franciscans, Dominicans, Mercedarians, or others. Some 150 young men were enrolled then in the major seminaries and about 200 in minor seminaries. About fifty Peruvian seminarians and priests are studying in Rome and twenty-five training in the U. S., Canada, or other European seminaries. With about 6,500 Peruvian youth sent abroad annually for college educations their ratio is about one hundred to one above those who plan to work exclusively for Christ. The number of priests in Peru, about 2050 during our tenure, has increased in the past two years. Of the 2050, more than half are in religious communities. About fifty percent of all the priests in Peru are from foreign soil.

"The public's image of the Church is radically changing," says Father Mallon. "We have a long way to go, but progress is being made. To give one brief statistic: One parish in Lima that ten years ago had 350 people going to Sunday Mass, today has more than 7,000 attending Sunday Masses and there is an average of 7,500 Holy Communions a month."

Too many Latin Americans believe that because the Roman Catholic religion is the official religion of some governments (Peru included) the government pays the Church's way. But it doesn't. Only Peru's Cardinal and her bishops receive monthly government stipends for church work. The amount for Cardinal Landazuri in the early 1960's was the equivalent of about $95; bishops received about $57.

Masses, funerals, baptisms, and wedding stipends ostensibly provide the income of the diocesan priests. However, many couples put off the church wedding and begin to live together after the civil wedding and the priest waits for that stipend while illegitimacy figures rise. No wonder the gringo is surprised, then, as we were near Chimbote in a little hacienda parish, when during an interview the priest told his young lay helper to bring out two roosters. "But don't put the knives on their feet," he cautioned. The fight was to be a training bout. For several minutes Luis Villares and I watched, took pictures and notes as two fighting cocks flew at each other in rage. The following weekend the priest had his fighters in the city hoping to pick up some extra money for himself and his parish. In Peru, cock fighting, like prostitution, is legal.

Some Latins, making no effort themselves to lead Catholic lives, will slander the Church, and to the newcomer this is shocking; but now and then we also encountered a Yankee who did likewise. One Midwesterner during a Hotel Bolivar reception remarked in the hearing of Catholics, and non-Catholics and to the embarrassment of PVs: "Isn't it a very liberal church down here? Don't priests have wives and families?"

Patronal thinking in the minds of some of the Church's affluent members has continued from colonial days. Today there are those among the oligarchy who welcome continued foreign aid because it relieves them of their obligations to their countrymen, whom they have neglected for generations, or when they did give some small aid, did so in a patronizing way.

Aware of this social injustice that has come down through the centuries, the foreigner, whether he is in religious life, lay mission work, or private enterprise, listens with interest, for example, to the words of Cardinal Cushing at the dedication of a new church in Comas Alta. The Boston prelate spoke in August of 1964 at the new St. James the Apostle church in the great slum complex. The Cardinal's nephew, Rev. William C. Francis, was named first pastor of the new parish that relieved some of the overload for nearby Canadian Oblates of Mary Immaculate. Four Sunday Masses in the former small, clapboard mission chapel razed to make way for the new church, brought in a total of two dollars in plate collections, a factor that guided Cardinal Cushing's decision to finance the new church, social welfare office, health clinic, and rectory.

"Don't blame the Church for the miserable conditions under which you have to live," the Boston prelate told Comas Alta residents through an interpreter. "No doctrine of the Church puts the stamp of approval on such social conditions. You can change it in a peaceful way. Elect people who will follow the encyclicals of the Popes of the past 75 years. You have a government willing to cooperate with the Alliance for Progress set up by President Kennedy. I have given the money for this church. No visitor will be able to say that we have asked money from the poor," the Cardinal said.

Looking about at wealthy Peruvians drawn to the slums by the presence of Cardinals Cushing and Landazuri and Archbishop Carboni, I wondered when more of their countrymen would cooperate in aiding the suppressed thousands. And those masses of neglected people in Comas and elsewhere — if a workable program of just wages, reduction of illiteracy, and development of social welfare advances one day brings aid and comfort to them, will they begin to contribute to national and Church betterment? Or will they follow the pattern of selfishness they have seen for generations?

While the Alliance for Progress, Agency for International Development, Peace Corps, and like programs from other foreign lands attempt to keep Latins as friends, the work of religious organizations, Catholic and non-Catholic alike, keeps many heads from turning toward atheistic communism.

At a reception welcoming Papal Volunteers, Cardinal Landazuri, though recognizing increased aid for the Church in Latin America, painted no gay picture: "Our problems are still monumental and the optimism we feel in the Latin American Church should not lull us into a fatal complacency." His Eminence didn't hesitate to point to the ground gained, speaking with pride about ten academically-approved seminaries opened in the past five years. Parish schools were unknown in Peru in the early 1950's; today, several dozens of them in Lima bolster the program of Catholic education. In Arequipa, Tacna, Piura, Puno, Iquitos, and other places the parish school idea grows.

But the complacency that Cardinal Landazuri warned about does exist; the Catholic layman from the U. S. and elsewhere is not doing his proportionate share in Latin American Church revitalization. The goal PAVLA originally set for volunteers in the field by 1965 was not reached; it was between 75 and 100 short of the 500 volunteers sought.

Peru, with her eleven million people in 1965, was in real need of spiritual re-enforcements; but what greater requirements will there be at the turn of the century when Lima (with approximately two million people now) will have from nine to twelve million as some demographers estimate?

For the rebuilding Church, improvements cited by Cardinal Landazuri will see some gains through Serra International, growth which will help foster native vocations, the Christian Family Movement to strengthen family life, and *Cursillos de Cristiandad* (Short

Course of Christianity) to inspire spiritual zeal among the Latins.

Amid some of this growth in a little cluster of parish buildings in the notorious Comas Alta slums, I watched a tank truck back up to a large barrel outside a low-roofed fiberboard building. The driver filled the barrel with water which required boiling to make it safe for drinking; he received five soles from the priest and was off to his next customer, another eighteen-cent sale for a two-day supply of water for shaving, Mass use, cooking, laundry . . . but hardly to quench one's thirst in the warm, dusty settlement.

"Why do these people crowd into such places?" I asked Father Francis.

"Despite the slum conditions the people feel that the little square of land here, on which they are continually adding to makeshift homes, is their own possession. Laboring for the hacienda owner in the hills, there was little that they could call their own," he said.

Down the sloping, rocky road about a mile west of St. James parish Canadian nuns operate Father Godin's social assistance clinic and a school for girls, with Papal Volunteers involved in the clinic and social service offices. The weekly begging trip of one of the nuns takes her into the wealthy districts of Lima. At one estate surrounded by a block-square high fence she was greeted on one of her trips by a muchacha who carried the sister's begging plea to the dama of the mansion. Returning moments later to the nun who had been left waiting outside the high gate, the muchacha said:

"Señora says your church has enough money."

Thereupon, the nun pointed out how her order struggles to buy medicines and begs from Canada and the U. S. for Comas' people.

"Tell her the money is not for us but for her neglected countrymen."

Back at the gate again the muchacha slid open the peek-a-boo door from behind the protective iron grating and replied:

"Señora says that she is Spanish. These are not her people!"

The little French-Canadian nun replied:

"Maybe she isn't Peruvian, or maybe she doesn't want to be Peruvian, but she made her wealth through the labors of these Peruvians, some of whom are living in Comas slums right now! Tell the dama not to forget that. Because God won't!"

And she departed.

Such age-old thinking that remnants of the oligarchy cling to no longer fills in for an alibi — if it ever did. And the Church herself must work toward updating the spirit of the recent Council, revamping her patterns of hairshirt, Middle-Age customs. One Peruvian woman emotionally reminded us of this, then told us her story.

On a Saturday afternoon years ago as she left a confessional in her parish, she fell in a cold faint. In the coffee-klatch session in our apartment she told us how her father, who was not practicing his religion, had forbidden her to go to Sunday Mass three weeks in a row. When she told her confessor this, his reply was: "Only the Pope can forgive this!" Leaving the confessional and childishly realizing that she would never be able to "go to Rome," she collapsed on the floor. Several women helped her outdoors and the priest, hearing the commotion, rushed up as she was revived. "He told me I should come back in and could receive absolution there," the woman recalled, 22 years after the incident.

Such attitudes, still fresh in some Latin's memories, hold back their spiritual development. Adela, the girl we met along Coronel Inclan streets when we arrived in Peru, was one with strong prejudices against the Church which could not be dislodged by the truth. In the Andean hills, too, strange legends and pagan practices, still clung to, stymie spiritual growth among the unschooled Indians. Centuries ago, for example, they were told that God likes to see His children happy and dancing. But many go overboard in revelry when the fiesta spirit is upon them and the drinks flow; they forget that God has also suggested, through the Beatitudes, that there is another type of happiness in His service.

Even on busy city streets one can find challenges to his faith from most unsuspected sources. On the Avenida Arequipa bus one afternoon the petite senior citizen sitting beside me struck up a conversation while handing me a little Gospel tract printed in English. The thicker packet she held was printed in Spanish.

"I've been doing the work of Jesus almost 25 years now in Peru," she said. "I used to live in Chicago."

In reply I briefly explained some of our PAVLA projects. Then our conversation switched to the weather which was trying to break away from winter into spring.

"When spring comes to Lima," the kindly woman went on, "people are too quick about changing from heavy underwear to summer underwear. Then they catch the grippe. And they're sick and sorry."

The grippe is Lima's seasonal change bugaboo. Surprising as it seemed, the Peruvians changing underwear too soon was symbolic of those Latins changing from their Catholic religion, better suited to their spiritual climate because of their baptism, to Protestant sects that may come along at any moment. They shed Catholicism before knowing its significance. Although about 94 percent of Latin America's people are baptized Catholics, the Protestant denominations have been busy for years, gaining followers as they go. Cardinal Cushing estimates that a million Latin American Catholics could be lost yearly, not necessarily to another faith, but just from Catholicism. Others in outlying areas have no opportunity to practice it. Because of this the Church has a monumental challenge ahead to develop a firm faith in people it can reach. After so long a period of neglect of body as well as soul, the task will not be easy.

Meanwhile, of pioneer Protestant denominations at Latin American mission posts, Britain's Anglican Communion — on the continent since cessation of our Civil War — had missioners stationed in remote Tierra del Fuego at the southern tip of South America, where their first dedicated people died of starvation while working with primitive Indians.

In Iquitos, the northeast Peru jungle city of some 65,000 people, we visited *Clinica Stahl* on the banks of the Amazon river. It is operated by Seventh Day Adventists whose German evangelists opened the mission in 1920. One of their U. S. doctors guided us on an interesting Sunday afternoon tour of clinic, social welfare offices, and the U. S. and Peruvian missioners' homes. Caring for the ailing, tending wounds, the clinic personnel are doing much for suffering mankind. Next to the church where their faith is nurtured, we saw Peruvian family groups picnicking while a lively volleyball game went on between North and South Americans.

As we walked along the road from the clinic, a North American stopped his jeep and offered us a lift to town; the jeep had a New Jersey license plate on it. As we drove along, the Amazon river amphibian just arriving on the weekly flight from Manaus, Brazil, winged in low for a landing.

"I'm a Baptist minister," the friendly Jerseyite said. "Came in for supplies. My family and I are working down river. Are you vacationing here?"

"Yes," we replied, and we told him about PAVLA.

What are the Protestant sects accomplishing in Peru? Personnel of the General Conference of the Seventh Day Adventists in Washington, D. C., offered some answers. They have been in Peru about fifty years and have 106 organized churches currently active. The smaller churches are financed usually by the local congregation but churches in larger cities are constructed with help from the General Conference in addition to local funds. The majority of the Adventist missionaries are married couples assigned to Latin America for five year periods, with nine-month furloughs between assignments. Their 1964 progress report showed twenty-six missionaries from the states in Peru while 421 Peruvians assisted their programs. "The number remains more or less constant except for a slight increase annually as the church grows," an official said. In 1964 Adventist membership in Peru was at 21,914, with a Sabbath School membership of 26,320. Many in the latter category are non-baptized members, accounting for the numerical difference.

Not many weeks after we arrived in Peru, Mary Ellen and I talked with a middle-aged Peruvian woman whom we passed daily on the way to Santa Maria Reina church, greeting her at the same corner at almost precisely the same time.

"I thought you were Mormon missioners, carrying your Bibles to work," said the woman, a member of the Seventh Day Adventist church. Our St. Joseph missals had linked us with Mormon missioners on their door-to-door visits for converts. Catholic Peru! But curiously and sadly enough, one of her citizen's first impressions about us concerned not the nation's Catholic faith at all! The Mormons, it should be stated, first organized their Andean Mission officially in 1959 although Mormons have been at work in Lima since 1956. Their Lima

Andean Mission office personnel report that they have 7,000 members in thirty-five churches scattered throughout major cities and small villages in the territory of Colombia, Ecuador, Peru, Bolivia, and Arica, Chile. Baptisms total about 1,500 annually. In Trujillo, one of Peru's larger coastal cities 340 miles north of Lima, the Mormons, with a membership of 117, launched a Boy Scout program. Like the Seventh Day Adventists, Mormons select promising young Latin Americans from their membership for study at Brigham Young University in Utah. Three of the Mormons' Andean Mission chapels are in Peru. Five were under construction in late 1965 with three more begun in 1966, financed by tithing from members. Their U. S. missionaries serve without pay, their food and clothing needs met by local members; transportation to and from the missions is financed by their parents. Young men and women train at the Mormon's language Training Institute on the Provo campus where intensified Spanish and scripture courses are offered.

In our movements within Peru, Bolivia, and Brazil we noted other Protestant missioners' activity.

In Viachi, a little community just north of La Paz, Bolivia, priests from the Archdiocese of St. Louis are busy, as are several St. Louis Papal Volunteers who came out from Christ the King parish in La Paz. Awaiting the two-car motor train in Viachi station, I walked a half block to a little food stall and spent eighteen Peruvian cents for a half dozen oranges and one unleavened bread roll about as round and flat as a saucer but rather tasty. I unhurriedly munched the bread and ate two of the oranges; at that 13,000-foot altitude I was one sea level PV who didn't sprint around the countryside like a native or veteran altiplano missioner, using caution to avoid soroche, mountain sickness. And going slowly for me up there even meant chewing my food that way. With these things in mind I looked across the street and noticed the Salvation Army home for children.

This was religion's story, Catholic and Protestant, unfolding for us in Latin America. Many, many Latins passing in front of Catholic churches outwardly show allegiance reflecting some faith within. You see it in the man in civilian clothes who makes the Sign of the Cross when he passes near a church and you wonder if he is a regular

Sunday Mass attender. It is true that many will make the Sign of the Cross when they pass a church even if they never enter one. The man in military uniform passes and salutes in the direction of the tabernacle and you feel that he could not be one of the men with two or three families to support. The ragged woman in the derby-type hat passes the church, looks beyond the open doors and tips her derby toward the altar. Is she one of the thousands of women whose men ran out on them? Along a path leading from a small Andean town we walked with a man who made ceramics in his little home outside town. As we walked, the man bent over quickly and plucked wild flowers, hardly interrupting the conversation. After several twists and turns of the footpath we came upon a small wayside shrine containing a weathered statue of the Virgin. Running on ahead, the Peruvian artist placed the flowers in front of the statue, then blessed himself. In a Lima television station, just before the Catholic Information Center's "Appointment with the Cardinal" program featuring the return of Cardinal Landazuri from the second session of the Vatican Council, the Peruvian moderator straightened his tie, ran his hand over his slick, black hair, blessed himself hurriedly, then walked out in front of the lights. During 1962 which Peru dedicated to her newest saint, some of her people prayed:

"O, glorious St. Martin de Porres! Intercede before the Lord for all of us, your compatriots. Help us to be each day more humble, charitable, and just. Pray to God for union and peace, for progress and happiness for our country, Peru, and all the world."

Occasionally, a person in public life renounces the spotlight for religious life as did José Mojica, Mexican-born singer who starred for fifteen years with the Chicago Grand Opera before the era of sound movies, then went to Hollywood for singing leads in films. His contemporaries were Ramon Navarro and Tony Moreno with Mona Maris and Conchita Montenegro as leading ladies, all of them high on the fans' popularity polls when the new "talkies" were the rage. When, as a bachelor in his early forties, life along the Great White Way suddenly appeared as something "carnival-like" to him, José Mojica in 1940 entered a Franciscan monastery in Lima. Shortly before we were to leave Peru, Mary Ellen and I chatted with Fray José

Francisco de Guadalupe Mojica next to a stamp window in Lima's general post office and the man whose signature was craved by fans who'd seen him in "King of the Gypsies," "Captain of the Cossacks," and other plays, was an inspiration to us. We told him of our pleasure at hearing him sing in Chimbote two nights before the assassination of President Kennedy while he was on a national tour raising funds for a new Franciscan seminary. That the Church in Latin America is reawakening is due in no little part to efforts of a man of God like Fray Mojica. Amid glaring Latin contrasts, Fray Mojica is one clergyman at once welcomed into the president's palace to assist at a fashionable wedding, or summoned to monastery waiting rooms to find a sobbing, aging woman whose tired hands slip rosary beads between her fingers as she talks. To the wealthy or to the forgotten, the blessing of Christ he imparts is no different. (Fray José de Guadalupe has since returned to his native land and has some 80 Mexican orphans under his care at San Miguel de Allende. He also encourages delayed vocations among men who wish to follow his example.)

For contrasts we think of the bus journey through the mountains when another priest boarded carrying a dusty, strap-style leather brief case with buckles hitched on either side of the unlocked fastener. In his other hand was a black umbrella he closed as he stepped inside from the hot, early afternoon sun. His wide-brimmed, flat black clergyman's hat was the type seen most often in St. Peter's square in Rome. The hat, like his faded black cassock with about half the buttons unfastened, was gray with dust. The priest looked about seventy years old. Neither passengers nor the conductor who collected his eight cent fare spoke a word or nodded to him as he shuffled to a vacant seat just across from us. "Good afternoon, Father," we said. Somewhat surprised, the elderly priest looked across and smiled. He was on his way to a Peruvian public school to teach afternoon catechism classes as the law provided. "You're not Peace Corps workers?" he inquired. When we said no, he continued talking: "I have to teach to help buy my food and clothes," he said, adding, too, how often he had wished that those many hours in the catechism classes could have been spent with people in the parish. "Maybe today the parish would have more members, maybe they'd understand more about church support. Maybe

I'm training youths who will help the priest that succeeds me," he said. Like humans the world over, people turn their heads when a Fray Mojica walks among them. They will gather to hear him sing. And this is understandable. But when the village priest boards the bus outside the limits of a far off mountain village, nobody nods, conversations continue without a split-second break for a smile, a cordial greeting; yet, each new day arriving in Lima or the mountains finds both men absorbed in the miracle of the Mass in his respective church, each unconcerned whether thousands or nobody says hello.

The Church advances, nevertheless, and even the simplest Sunday bulletin from the slum parish carries a detail of this story. Activities are spelled out plainly for those of limited education. There's the quarter page devoted to matrimony, the two plain rings interlocked with a cross carrying the message: "Man — Woman, United Before God." There's the report of 37 weddings, most of them of couples from the hills who had completed the civil wedding years ago. (So it was not unusual that one to a half dozen of their children attended the church ceremony). Elsewhere in the bulletin are notes that a volunteer doctor is at the parish from three to six o'clock every Saturday afternoon; a lawyer is there Sunday mornings offering free legal aid; Sunday nights the Girls for Catholic Action hold weekly meetings; literacy classes are Monday and Thursday afternoons for the women.

Essential as the Church and the Mass are in the lives of the people, one cannot overlook the tremendous material want. Speaking to Catholic Medical Mission personnel during an annual conference in Arequipa, Dr. Arnoldo Valdavia, then president of the Peruvian-North American Medical Association of Arequipa, praised the new look of the Catholic Church in altering its past contemplative attitude, drawing toward positive solutions of the problems of hunger, thirst, and pain. "It is a ray of light to people who suffer and wait," Dr. Valdavia said.

No one understands such suffering and waiting any better than those victims, either suppressed by former rulers of Peru or today's miserable ones in the slums, who for years have been singing about it in their Peruvian National Anthem:

A long time the Peruvian was oppressed,
held down by the ominous chain,
condemned by cruel servitude,
a long time, a long time
in silence he moaned.

In downtown Lima's La Merced Church one finds a very interesting wall upon entering the over-ornamented facade fronting on
Jirón Unión. La Merced dates back to 1534. The Peruvian devotion
to Our Lady of Mercy began in 1615 when Limaneans sought her
intercession against the danger that Dutch Corsairs along the South
American coast might invade Lima, vanquish the Spaniards, and
Peru would have a new ruler suppressing her. On September 24, Peruvians observe the national holiday of Our Lady of Mercy which had its
beginnings in 1821, the year of their independence from Spain when
General José San Martín made her Marshal of the Peruvian Army, a
title she still holds. In a little cubicle at the back of the church is a
painting of Christ crucified. In place of the usual crown of thorns there
is a crown of silver, fashioned with the metal obtained from remelting
of silver heart-shaped gifts people bring to the church, gifts which
Adela told us months earlier were to go, she thought, to Vatican City.

Adela's countrymen approached this wall and petitions from fast-
moving lips poured forth. Many petitions were written on that wall
with pencil or ball-point pen. And at least three times during my
observations the wall was covered with petitions, then repainted. Little
by little the messages reappeared, neatly written, printed, or shakily
scribbled. A few were in English. While I stood back copying several
of the messages on the back of an envelope, a wizened, bent little
woman, lighted candle in one hand, reached toward the candle rack,
half watching what she was doing and half interested, it seemed, in
why I was writing my petition on paper. "Don't you know you must
write it on the wall to get best results?" I supposed her to be thinking as I copied:

"Please help me in my solitude."

"Lord, help my son that he may pay his bills."

"Lord, cure me. I am sick. Thank you. Amen."

One message was incomplete. It began, "Lord, help my wife—."

Perhaps one of the Mercedarian priests or brothers who made rounds regularly in the great church (with its fourteen large side altars in addition to the grand main altar) interrupted the petitioner.

And another with marital significance:

"Lord, help me with problems of my soul and that of my husband, Humberto, that he will return to me and that we will lack nothing."

One petitioner had a struggle with her English, as her message revealed:

"Please, God, I want to become in another way of life, behaving myself very well. Help me, your daughter."

On the lime-colored wall near the edge of the painting I read:

"Lord, Jesus . . . please help me to buy a welding machine for my house," penned by some petitioner who hoped perhaps to start a home industry with dreams of improved material needs.

High Mass at the far end of the columned church was under way when I slipped the envelope into my pocket and left the alcove. Leaving the church, I felt a tug at my sleeve.

"Señor . . . lottery ticket? Last one! Good luck! Win 10,000 soles Saturday!"

"No thanks."

But never mind, the lottery salesman will sell that "last one," make the Sign of the Cross of thanksgiving in front of La Merced, then reach into his inside pocket and bring out another "last one" that people buy for luck. It's good business to stand outside La Merced, selling lottery tickets.

CHAPTER X

THROUGH ANXIOUS TIMES

Twenty-four hours after the news of President Kennedy's death had reached us, I was in Lima's massive, nineteenth-century post office, my mind clogged with painful thoughts of the assassination of our President.

A slight, moustached Peruvian approached me. "You are from the United States?" he asked. "Sí Señor." And this stranger's arms enfolded me in an abrazo; he had nothing but "deep sorrow for the people in your nation because of the wrong committed in the city of Dallas." He spoke of his sadness "for the Kennedy family, for Jacqueline, for the children." In the distance, atop the 22-story modern Ministry of Education building the red and white Peruvian flag was flying at half mast as were all the banners in a city awaiting the official day of mourning the following Monday.

Had the stranger before me been my dearest friend and the victim been my brother, the man's expression of sincerity duplicated over and over by so many Peruvians meeting "Los Yanquis" during those hours, could not have been more sincere or more appreciated. The C.I.C. secretary with tears welling in her eyes told us the awful news five hours after it happened as we returned from a six-hour road trip to Chimbote on office assignment. There was no radio in the car so Luis Villares and I entered the office unaware.

It was hard at first to understand the meaning of the "pop, pop, pop!" some youths were making on the streets until I heard one of them say with a sneer as I left the post office:

"Todos los Yanquis! Pop, pop, pop!"

Like crashing cymbals the message came through . . . pop, pop, pop
. . . three shots were fired in Texas. And one young Peruvian was
suggesting that there should be similar shots for "all the Yankees."

Across from the post office I awaited a bus marked "Matute" while
at the opposite curb the noisy ones hovered around two motorbikes
watching the "Yanqui" on the other side. Theirs was the only evidence of such an attitude I encountered.

This incident might be viewed as an indicator of how suddenly
life in Latin American lands can shift from the serene to the agitated.
I walk through the plaza one day and the Civil Guard policeman is
covering his assigned post in cloth peaked cap, green uniform, and
truncheon. Any tension is miles away. Next day, in the same plaza
the officer on duty wears his steel protective helmet, very much at the
ready, always looking about, keeping people moving, allowing no
groups to form. The rochabus (riot vehicle that cools off people with
strong streams of water during demonstrations) is parked a half
block down the street, engine running. A squad of Civil Guard assault troops stands at ease on another corner. Though a Papal Volunteer, to 99 out of 100 people I'm a foreigner first, furthermore a
Yankee — automatically super rich. If trouble erupts in the streets,
discretion tells me to stay out of the way until tempers cool. This is
their country, their business. Some of the agitators may not be happy
until vengeance spills over from the grievance at hand to "rich"
gringos, or shoeshine boys, or socialites. It's surprising where, why,
and how trouble can explode into the open so quickly.

Considering anxiety complexes, bad luck omens, and the like, it
was interesting to learn that Peruvians regard any Sunday the 7th
with the same legendary and cautious concern that we give to Friday
the 13th. They seriously considered Sundays dated the 7th in 1962,
1963, and 1964. "Be careful, Sunday the 7th!" Peruvians will say.
They tell the aging tale of the elderly lady who was the model of
caution on Sunday the 7th; she never left the house, but there was the
Sunday the 7th that a horse became frightened in the street and bolted
right into her house, stampeded wildly around the room and trampled
the woman to death.

Worrying about Friday the 13th and Sunday the 7th, and the possibilities of explosive national crises in between, a person never would get his job done in Latin America. Regardless of the acute bus shortage in most large cities, and the deplorable condition of some of the rolling stock, there are fanatics who during a disturbance will lob a Molotov cocktail in or under a bus. During bus strike tension, for example, one important, free-riding passenger is the policeman sitting just behind the driver holding his rifle ready for trouble. But we could not fret too much about yesterday's newspaper picture of a burned-out bus in the street, or we never would get across town to work. The morning following the May 24, 1964, stadium tragedy we passed a burned-out bus from our line at the National Stadium corner. There it remained until Peruvians had buried more than 300 dead, treated the injured in hospitals, and repaired business buildings in the vicinity of the stadium that were damaged when the soccer fans carried their riot from the tear-gas choked stadium into the streets.

Like communism, such anxieties are there under the surface as a potential danger. Gringos normally don't go down to Plaza San Martin for an F.L.N. (National Liberation Front) Red rally. And curiously enough, the only Russian citizens I was certain that I saw in Peru during our three years were two comrades walking along Avenida Nicolas de Pierola, more popularly known as La Colmena, "the beehive," because of its constant, hurry-scurry in-town pace. They were members of Russia's touring soccer team and wore distinctive matched sports jackets with identifying "CCCP" pocket patches.

That times are not as troublesome in Peru as they might be can be attributed to the late nineteenth-century effectiveness of President Nicolas de Pierola, for whom Lima's "beehive" is named. In 1895 he began four years of successful government which reinforced economic stability, brought about feelings of confidence and security in the people, and moved the nation to undertake new institutional enterprises, new development in trade with other nations. Threescore years after Nicolas de Pierola made his indelible mark on Peruvian history, my wife and I were to hear his daughter-in-law, Mrs. Victoria (Hancock) de Pierola, tell us:

"It was my husband's father who stood in the Senate of Peru and told members that 'our problems are nothing now. Wait until the day people begin to understand their rights and what is due them as human beings.'" We had gone to Mrs. de Pierola's in-town apartment with a priest, who wanted us to help him persuade her to move from her apartment to a nursing home where she would have professional care. The maiden name "Hancock" of the elderly socialite, who was born in Chicago, meant that she was a direct descendant of the first signer of the Declaration of Independence.

Upon her arrival in Lima in the early 1920's, the Chicagoan was thrilled during Sunday afternoon rides with her husband in the four-wheeled victoria pleasure carriage with its calash top thrown back. People stared at them, as they drove along Unión out to Paseo Colon, a gringa dama with her Peruvian spouse. Many brown eyes fixed upon her fair hair, fair skin. Admittedly, she wanted to see the Peruvians equally as much; but she recalled for us that when she did on one occasion steal a furtive glance, her husband politely admonished her:

"Cara frente!"

Face the front, look straight ahead not curiously to either side. Her position must be remembered always. It was. As age came upon her and illness, she was quite alone in her apartment, drawn blinds shutting out the gray, misty day. We marveled. How doggedly has the "cara frente" posture held up during generations of Latin American exclusive elegance!

"Oh, but we fed the poor years ago, too," she said with the bed covers drawn up to her chin. "We served breakfast to the poor every day. Not like today's powdered milk and one bread roll. There was orange juice and toast and eggs. . . ."

"How many did you feed daily?" Mary Ellen asked, but there was no answer, only more information brought back from another era.

"I was active in seven or eight clubs, always busy," she recalled. We heard how prize asparagus from Belgium was done up by her in attractive red and white ribbons, "colors of Peru, you know," and presented to her friends in government and at the archbishop's palace. She pointed to the night stand where lay a watch her husband had given her for a wedding present. Looking at our own timepieces, and with nothing settled on her moving into a nursing home, we arose, bade farewell, and from that time on we saw more of the Peruvian culture more clearly. During our two remaining years there the "cara frente" phrase remained filed in our minds as the watchword of the oligarchs — Face front. Don't look for the misery or you'll see it.

How many people of means in Latin America, since days of vice-regal colonization, admonished their children with "cara frente"? How often did a son of the wealthy Peruvian bursting with fervor and faith of his first Holy Communion urge his parents to allow him to go to the seminary to become a priest? How often was he ridiculed, jokingly called "padre" or "cura," until his vocation succumbed to the system? How many children were sent to the private schools taught by priests and nuns with the understanding that after graduation they could dump that religion and take up the anti-clerical attitudes of their elders?

Of the 230 million people in Latin America, over ninety percent have been baptized Catholics. Yet, says one veteran missionary priest, Hispanic Catholicism "hasn't made their world livable for human beings." How many more priests are needed to serve the baptized Catholics? Some say 145,000 for all of Latin America, and 100,000 nuns and lay catechical instructors. As these numbers are approached, one wonders how much longer some of the colonial thinking about practicing Catholicism will prevail.

Juan Cardinal Landazuri Ricketts has repeatedly deplored conditions that spawned "enormous religious ignorance of the great masses of people." His Eminence, son of an esteemed Peruvian family of means, studied with the Franciscans in the monastery at Ocopa, just north of Huancayo located in the beautiful high sierra valley of the Mantaro river.

While on a Central Railway train passing near there one day we ourselves had a glimpse of the conditions breeding that ignorance. While the train stopped at San Jerónimo station early in the morning, we watched a front door open in an adobe hut across the tracks. A little girl ran out carrying her school bag and the door closed behind her. She was getting her chance for education. The door reopened, and out came a smaller girl, not in school, longingly watching her sister in the distance. Finally, the family pig nudged the door open with his snout and squeezed out into the sunlight for a day of foraging after spending the night indoors with the family. From the same dwelling a school bag and pork on the hoof. The symbol was plain.

Since that trip I've carried in my wallet a Peruvian five sol note (redeemable for about 18.6 cents U. S.) with "we will recover the oil!" rubber-stamped in purple ink along the note's smudged quarter-inch border. "Huancayo" is hand-printed in red ink on the lower edge. The bill is a keepsake reminder of Peru's sporadic agitation — sometimes initiated by the left wing press, always loudly advocated by Communist F.L.N. followers — to confiscate the foreign-owned, money-making oil industry in northern Peru, surrounding Talara by the sea, and place it under state ownership. On that carefree outing with Mary Ellen and other Papal Volunteers plus a couple visiting religious from Chicago and Brooklyn, some of Peru's tensions cropped up, a situation which really took something away from the weekend of relaxation. (On another soiled border of my piece of paper money I inked in the date, June 22, 1963.)

Outside the Huancayo cathedral that Sunday morning we were happy to see young men involved in Church-orientated work. On their right arms they wore sleeve bands displaying the initials "A.C.P." — Peruvian Catholic Action. The young men can be compared to those in Catholic Youth Organizations or Youth For Christ in this nation. Greeting people leaving the ancient cathedral, they were asking donations for construction of a boys' primary school. These were not indeed the ones shouting for oil confiscation as they pinned "pro construcción" tags on our coats. Two days after Cardinal Giovanni Battista Montini was elected on the fifth ballot, taking the name Paul VI as spiritual leader of the world's 585 million Catholics, high in the Andes we saw some Church gains, but the Peruvian sol note in my wallet constantly reminds us that any continued progress ahead won't be a piece of cake.

Communist guerrillas plagued Peru when we were there, and the civil police combed the hills 190 miles east of Lima in the Department of Junin, where Huancayo is the capital. At times national anti-guerrilla forces up to 1500 in number, some of them trained at U. S. bases, ferreted out Red terrorists, some of whom were insurrection-trained in Cuba. News accounts reported that a handful of the big boys in the guerrilla camps had roamed rice paddies with the Viet Cong, picking up some of their skill under Far East Reds. Those Red guerrillas operated in four separate bands, claiming an aggregate of no more than 1,000 members. Junin's hills have been reported to be a stronghold of Communist rebels who stir up the campesinos, but valleys leading into Cuzco, some 500 mountainous miles to the southeast, were also points of Red operations. President Belaunde once referred to the guerrillas as "cattle rustlers, that's all." But his administration has been keeping good tab on them, spoiling any plans to enlarge their operations; there has been no widescale linking up of Indians with Red bands; in the main they have not responded to agitation geared for popular uprisings spurred on by "Land or Death" chants. Peruvians note that such agitation isn't confined to the hills among the un-schooled campesinos. Activities traceable to the Communist front erupted in Lima as recently as July, 1965, when three hours after midnight an employee of the Hotel Crillon hastily retrieved a package thrown into the lobby and tossed it onto the pavement of Avenida Nicolas de Pierola, fronting on the hotel entrance. The concealed bomb exploded, shattering windows on both sides of the streets and bending a section of the streetcar tracks. In the hotel one always finds patrons from foreign lands, not a few of them from the United States, and the July 4 bomb plant has implications that the Red terrorists wanted to claim some "Yankees." That day the government began another roundup of known Communists.

In a nation where a shortage of religious is so acute the government, during one Red roundup, was relentless in its search for a man wearing the cassock of the Catholic church's priesthood. A search for the suspended Padre Salomon Bolo Hidalgo was front-page copy. His activities had been the model of confusion ever since 1945 when he was attracted to the Dominican order and began studying for the priesthood, a goal to prove unattainable in that religious community. The same member of Peru's hierarchy who ordained him later for the diocesan priesthood in 1958, Bishop Teodosio Moreno Quintana, of Huaraz (a mountain city of about 28,000 people some 250 miles northeast of Lima), also suspended Bolo in 1962 for pro-communist activities. Following ordination Padre Bolo became an Army chaplain, later being dismissed for failure to obey superiors plus scandalous conduct, the latter charge based on his living with a married woman in the northern frontier town of Tumbes. Returned to proper priestly life, Padre Bolo drew a real "Siberia" assignment, deep in the hills of the Huaraz diocese at Navcos, where he became pastor. Even in such remote surroundings the unpredictable padre found himself in trouble again. His pastoral yen to make parish changes included the authorization for a large mural for one of the church walls, showing two Hells: one was a pleasant, beautiful place where Stalin, Hitler, and Khrushchev resided; the other, a very bad place, was for all capitalists. Complaints on this were coupled with objections of fervent parishoners to his association with the Commie director of a public school and charges that he was teaching heresy. F.L.N. party campaigns of 1962 and 1963 to get their Red candidates into office flopped, along with Bolo's feverish bid to become one of the nation's vice-presidents. During heated pre-1962 election campaigning townspeople in the Seven Corners district of Arequipa hung Padre Bolo in effigy, then lowered their dummy dressed in pajamas, and burned it — the Church had forbidden Bolo to wear his cassock (although he continued to do so). Some Arequipaneans conduct an annual Holy Week ceremony in which Judas is hung and burned; that year, the figure of the traitor-apostle was replaced in the plaza ceremony by that of the suspended clergyman.

During tense, national times Papal Volunteers, for the most part, were occupied in areas away from the disturbances. There was the exception in Sicuani when the volunteers, overtaxed in an overcrowded hospital, tended the injuries of country people — men, women, and children — injured in a flareup between police and Communists, the latter having stirred up the farmers in another brief bid for revolution. On leave at the PAVLA regional center in Lima after the fighting, PVs told how the victims were placed on flatcars outside Sicuani where the skirmish took place and brought to the hospital, where nurses and hospital personnel had to go among the bodies to determine those still alive. Witnesses of the clash reported that the women and children were put in the front lines as the two "armies" closed for battle. Men who were strangers to the Sicuani community, those out of the Cuzco communist cells, stayed in the background chanting the "Land or Death" slogan of the F.L.N. The innocent died and were maimed, not the outside agitators. Unfortunately, the illiterate hill Indians would always be in the front lines, carrying banners of anarchy they could not read. They would throw in with anyone who promised them better days.

Such a misguided person who had been brainwashed by the F.L.N. was young Pedro, who used the public playground in the park surrounding Our Lady of Guadalupe parish as his forum for preaching anarchy, condemning the parish priests and the Church, showing disdain for the military junta, for jabs at democracy, and cheers for Castro and Khrushchev. The first time nineteen-year-old Pedro and I talked on a late Sunday afternoon, he was dog-trotting across the park, returning from a soccer game. He carried his little cloth ditty bag. Earlier, several Papal Volunteers working with youth on that playground had commented on Pedro's cute ideas peddled to any listeners while executing his bagful of tricks on the parallel bars. As I watched Pedro slow up and move into the center of a group of boys, he dug into his bag and brought out a folded newspaper and began reading to them. I wondered: Was it something from *Obrero y Campesino*, the Trotskyite propaganda sheet printed in Lima urging "Working Class of the World, Unite!" (And there was always that hammer and sickle out on the front page, top corner.) *Obrero y Campesino*, along with *Frente, Revolución*, and a few others with Red platforms were fly-by-night sheets usually consisting of four pages without advertising. They were party propaganda rags, no more.

Innocently enough this time, Pedro was reading from a newspaper backed by one of the big three Peruvian politicos and his message was that on the coming Sunday there would be a huge, free bazaar sponsored by the politicos in Lima's Breña district. Fun, games, free pop for the kids . . . for the adults, some party promises. Pedro knew his business about letting the kids in on something free; next time he could read what the revolutionaries wanted spread.

The high school boys scattered over to where a soccer game was forming across the park oval. Little boys ran back to the swings and slippery slide; Pedro and I were the only ones around so he asked me what I was doing in Peru. He found out, and in answer to my question said: "No, I'm not a student. I'm saving money to go to the university if I'm accepted."

Many university-age men and women would like to continue their education, but crowded facilities and limited entrance opportunities keep them from such goals. In 1940 Peru had 3,843 university students on its few campuses. In 1960 statistics show the number had grown to some 18,000; since then facilities and enrollments have expanded but in 1960 only 17.6 persons in every 10,000 were university students in national institutions.

"How do you make your money?" I asked Pedro, wondering if any payola came his way from the party.

"I work in a telegraph office downtown," he said, then changed the subject. "We got a boys' club. Why not come over some night and do a story with pictures on us?" I didn't make any promises; a policeman from the Balconcillo district walked by and I exchanged greetings with him. The patrolman, whom I had called "jefe," was now out of earshot reading the riot act to several altiplano women and children for picking red and yellow canna blooms from the flower beds. Only weeks earlier the offshore winds had whipped dust off the bare, powdery park soil, and when enough pressure was brought to bear on the district officials, the park crew came out, hand-planted grass shoots, and laid out the beautiful canna beds. Now the unschooled from the hills were picking the new blossoms — not for their straw huts, of course, but to sell in the market. Rice in the bowl is more important to those people than flowers in a vase . . . a vase which they do not own anyway.

"You shouldn't call him jefe," Pedro blurted out. Jefe is almost unconsciously used in conversations with the taxi driver, the passing policeman, somebody in a public office, or maybe in a store. It means "chief" or "leader" and nine out of ten Latins, when you use it on them, puff up a bit.

"What's the matter with jefe?" I asked Pedro.

"Policemen are ignorant and don't know the difference."

"Difference about what?"

"People's rights, street directions. The difference between chief and workers."

About the street directions I couldn't present much of an argument. We remember how in a district city hall on the anniversary of the birth of Miguel Cervantes, we got such mixed up directions we never did get to see the wreath placed at his bust in a plaza named for him.

"Where do you hear this?"

"At meetings" — not saying what meetings. A split second later he was talking about Russia.

"Bueno. If Russia doesn't have freedom, at least the people have bread. In Peru we have liberty but no bread."

I thought about the four men seated at a sidewalk cafe table on the north side of Plaza San Martin; quite boisterous they were as empty beer bottles accumulated in front of them. It was two days after President Belaunde had taken office on July 28, 1963, ending a year and 10 days of military junta control. "Now we live in a free country again," the men shouted to passersby.

"Did you have your pancitos this morning, Pedro?"

"Yes, but many hungry people in the mountains didn't have bread. That's why they crowd into Lima . . . tired, homeless, sick and hungry."

When I mentioned the shipments of Caritas (Catholic Relief Service) foodstuffs distributed in Lima and the mountains, Pedro hurriedly interrupted to remind me such food was poor quality which the U. S. had rejected. (The Reds brought the gem out periodically, and one season they cried that the incoming clothing from the U. S. bishops' Thanksgiving relief drive was contaminated — that it was collected at hospitals from patients suffering from infectious diseases.)

"In Southeast Asian nations the Reds don't lie about the quality of the wheat, Pedro. They are just smart enough to put their Communist markings on the sacks so you don't see the names anymore of the free nations from which the foodstuffs come. They take credit for providing the food instead of being stupid about the quality of the products."

Pedro, remembering his leftist indoctrination — if you can't lie your way out of attacks against the "imperialists," change the subject — picked up where we had left off earlier, admitting the lack of liberty in Russia, admitting that he didn't like that idea.

"So, do the people living without freedom enjoy their bread, Pedro?"

No answer. Our conversation might have ended there but good old Pedro kept on until he was into the petroleum production in the north of Peru near the Ecuador frontier.

"Foreigners rob us of our resources," Pedro said, pointing out how for 50 years British and North Americans have been taking huge profits from Peru's raw materials. He agreed, however, that Peruvian workers in those refineries were among the best paid in his land, and yes, he had seen the full-page newspaper ad of that week where many workers signed a statement about the high wages after an opposing newspaper got out the editorial again about Peru's oil being for Peruvians, etc.

"But they use those good wages to buy beer, get drunk and their kids don't eat," Pedro said.

"Do you ever have a glass of beer?"

"I've had some, not anymore. Drinking beer is bad!"

"Why is it bad if a person drinks a glass of beer if he's man enough or smart enough to know his limit? Not knowing when to stop is the bad part, keeping money from the family to get drunk is the bad part. Ever heard of Russian vodka? Do you think your friends over there are lily-white sober?"

An offside soccer ball bounded toward us. Nimble Pedro whisked to his feet like a leaf swept from the turf by a gusty breeze and with a well-aimed kick sent it sailing back into the center of the game.

"A Communist's like the drunk who doesn't know when to quit — wants to enslave the world. Like Marx' dream," I said. "That Castro was the muy macho hero when he entered Havana but in a couple months the corner grocery stores were his, then the service stations,

Mountain woman at Puno, Peru, passes stall where young boys read comic books on sale. Note household enamelware in stall to right . . . Bolivian couple, south of La Paz, visits with New York Franciscan priest while harvesting coca leaf. Dangerous slopes are seen on distant mountainside fields . . . A tacora reed boat is being produced entirely by hand along Lake Titicaca shores, the highest navigable lake in the world (12,500 feet above sea level, in Andean mountains in southeast Peru).

On rare occasions one would come upon such crude signs in Lima. Papal Volunteers and most Peruvians pass them but don't believe them. (Who can believe a communist?) . . . Occasionally foreigners in Peru like to see their nation's flag. The United States embassy in central Lima provides this opportunity . . . Medical and dental aid for jungle residents near Iquitos, Peru, along the Amazon river, is provided by a Peruvian Air Force "flying clinic" . . . A month after President Kennedy's assassination, Peruvian and U. S. officials dedicated this memorial in Lima park done by an Arequipa artist. This work was the first in the world to be dedicated after the tragedy.

and the banks and hotels and church property owned and paid for by foreign religious groups. Castro's drunk with power, like the petroleum worker in Talara who can't handle a glass of beer and never should buy it. How do you like what Castro's done to a once-free Cuba?"

The ball bounded toward us again. This time Pedro picked it up and started carrying it back toward the game. In the fading afternoon sun he'd get in a little more exercise. "Hasta luego," he shouted back over his shoulder, going off without the usual handshake and adding: "Sorry you work for nothing for the church."

It was unfortunate that Pedro and Jorge Gonzales never met to swap ideas. Jorge could have opened the youth's eyes. Jorge was a Cuban lay teacher in a Canadian religious brothers' school until Castro's gang expelled the Canadians and took their property. Young Morales, a winning, likable, very handsome man, knows where the Catholic Action is, a trait that brought him out of Cuba with the brothers. For a short time he lived in Canada until his papers were cleared for the trip to Peru; then off he went to the land of the Incas where he was assigned to teach in a boy's technical school operated by the Canadian brothers at the west edge of the sprawling Comas slum. Eventually he collaborated with Papal Volunteers assigned to the Canadian Oblates of Mary Immaculate. PVs at Maryknoll's St. Rose of Lima parish in the Lince district of Lima arranged a PAVLA meeting and Jorge Morales helped spell out for us what Cubans in a free world are doing through Christian endeavors to oppose communism's tyranny.

Stomach flutterings, when sweeping the day's headlines on newsstands in Lima, came and went depending on how international developments happened to stir the local left-wing, tacky-looking press editions. During the missile showdown between President Kennedy and Khrushchev the four-page tabloid *Revolución* wanted the average reader to believe that World War III was about to be launched. In red ink, with EXTRA! across the top of page one, the tabloid screamed: "Russia Will Use Her Warlike Power In Violent, Total Defense of Cuba!" . . . and below: "Urgent Message of Nikita Kruschov." Across the bottom of page one in headline type: "The

People of Latin America are at the point of war against *los Amos Yanquis!*" (Now and then "Amos" appears as the Left-Wingers' de-meaning reference to Uncle Sam). *Revolución,* another paper of the irresponsible press, appears on no particular schedule, but whenever it's out you can paint it red, to borrow a phrase. The staff of another Red sheet, *Frente,* who banded together under the hammer and sickle to put out its irregularly appearing sheet was hypnotized by the hackneyed "Cuba, Sí, Yanquis, No," headline. And they habitually proclaimed "Long live the friendship of the People of Peru and Cuba!" Castro himself was often pictured in combat uniform ranting into a brace of microphones on one of his long harangues.

When a Cuban is the caliber of Jorge Morales, or thousands like him who fled the Reds, the free world most certainly joins in sup-port of one thing *Frente* cries: "Long live the friendship of Peru (and you could add Brazil, the U. S., Israel, and the free world) with the people of Cuba!"

During the presidential campaigns of 1962 and 1963 slogans painted on walls, sides of buildings, and appearing on banners strung across streets, constantly cried out the dire state of the nation's social welfare.

The Odria party promised health, education, and work — throwing the spotlight on the pitiful neglect in these matters for so many people in misery. The victorious Popular Action party shouted the slogan "Forward!" as they were giving the voters "facts, not words!" In the year and a half we observed the Belaundistas in the palace we could see signs in favor of programs to unshackle the nation from the strangling grip of the oligarchy. Peru on the march for everyone! The slogan of Victor Raul Haya de la Torre, Peru's perennial candidate but never a winner for his APRA (American Popular Revolutionary Alliance) party, was: "APRA, Sí — Communism, No!" Christian Democrats said they would have "Clean Hands" in their administration. And Communist Pando's followers insisted on "Cuba, Sí — Yankees, No!" Pando's pawns also wooed slum dwellers with the slogan: "Bread and Liberty!"

For U. S. citizens unschooled in Latin American politics, the sud-den thrust into their culture during a heated campaign is a bit bewildering, to say the least, like trying to figure out how the man in favor of one candidate will elbow into the opposition's crowd and cheer for his man in a land of quick tempers and emotions, or like trying to figure out the actions of Aprista boss Haya de la Torre. What a politically-hectic past he has had! During Peru's coup d'etat of General Odria, Haya went into hiding on January 3, 1949, when his party was outlawed after an Aprista-led revolt of Peruvian navy officers failed in Callao harbor. Haya scooted into the Columbian embassy. Latin America still recognizes political asylum, so Haya remained a political prisoner there until April 6, 1954 — five and a quarter years. His is one of the most famous political asylum cases in Latin American history. Despite International Court discussions in the Hague, the case went unsettled until Peru and Colombia agreed to give Haya safe conduct from Peru. Later, during Prado's second presidency, Haya was allowed back home where he is free to come and go now, arriving to rally his followers for party unity, party funds, then off again to Europe or the U. S. A. for speaking engagements.

Notwithstanding politics being as exciting as they are in Latin America, for everyone, Peruvian, Chinaman, Russian, atheist, Yankee, or the pious beata who spends much of her time in church — the real anxiety in Andean territory is El Terremoto, the earthquake! The common El Temblor is usually less violent, and does not result in death, injury, or any grave property damage. At the first shake of the earth, however, Latin Americans living in the vicinity of the Andes rush to open ground clear of possible falling objects. One plump cook in a Lima rectory is widely-known, when the room begins to shake and rattle, to flee not into the outdoors but rather toward the first priest she sees, to throw her arms around him and cry out: "Lord of the Miracles, Save Us!" Many people go beneath the arch of a doorway and stand there, hoping the belief that arches don't collapse holds true another time. One Papal Volunteer was observed hurrying toward the back of the church and outside during a temblor while his wife steadily, if not calmly, approached the communion rail. I was that fleeing PV.

During our first four Peruvian months, every time I went for a haircut (usually about fifteen cents in the neighborhood shops), there was a recorded temblor, or tremor, either that same day or the day after. For the sake of keeping the earth still I began thinking of doing without haircuts. In one six weeks' period of August-September 1963 people fretted during eleven real jello-like shakes. One shake jolted us during 7 o'clock Mass at Our Lady of Guadalupe parish. Genial Father Julian Resch was celebrant. He's the first Norbertine (Order of Canons Regular of Premontre) to arrive at the mission he founded, assigned by superiors from St. Norbert's Abbey, DePere, Wis. That first snap of the earth caused the windows to rattle in their casings, lights to sway, and walls to creak a bit under the strain, and brought us from our meditations just before Holy Communion. The whip-like movement eased into a steady, mild shake, its accompanying rumbling noises becoming less loud. Then another snap of the earth, more rumbles, and with that one, women raised their voices almost in unison, and arose, too, for the flight from the church imploring protection from Our Lord of the Miracles on the way out. Earthquakes create their own particular brand of fear. The late Father Charles McCarthy, M.M., told me about one of his Chilean earthquake experiences. "I felt the ground snap, the church tremble, and as I turned to go for the wine and water at the Offertory I saw both altar boys going out one of the side windows, cassocks flying!"

At the Guadalupe altar, I was told later, Father Julian held Host on high before distributing Holy Communion, just when Mary Ellen whispered to me after the first tremor, "Let's go . . ." After Mass I faced the issue squarely when she asked where I disappeared so fast. "But you said, 'Let's go!'" I told her. "With the building jumping around I knew you meant outside!"

Not exactly. She had started to say: "Let's go to Communion."

Going through the anxious moments on the PV beat, the volunteer sees the constant tug-of-war between wealth and poverty, the person working for the priest and the one working against him, and in time one has his share of emotion-packed scenes which present one of the distressing aspects of the work in which he has become involved. One never gets completely accustomed to the entire spectrum, but after awhile it's no trick to make a list of some of the things that Peruvians fear besides the earthquake. The abandoned mother in the barriada food line fears that the flour, cooking oil, or rice will be gone when her turn arrives. The office clerk or school boy running for the bus or streetcar fears he'll be crowded out, not only from a place to sit or stand inside the bus or car but even from a place to hang on outside somewhere near the rear door. Pious women surging to the Communion rail fear there will be a shortage of hosts, or on Palm Sunday they fear there'll be no palms. The sun returns to Lima after the misty winter and spring and people flocking to public beaches fear they won't get their places in the sun, sand, and surf.

In their day-to-day living many Peruvians don't expect buses on routes through poorer sections to be free of offensive, sickening fumes escaping faulty exhaust pipes. Even Mary Ellen wasn't overly excited that time a wheel of the rickety bus fell off on her way home from work. People don't expect to see a cover over every sewer because they would have no other place to throw their refuse that gathers in the corralons. If a driver, unfamiliar with the neighborhood, cracks into the sewer opening and breaks a wheel and perhaps several teeth, well, after all. . . . They expect public service offices to be crowded and they'll wait. They expect to make four or five trips to the general post office to pick up a parcel from overseas.

Papal Volunteers, as a part of that Latin American scene, expect to welcome the joys or share the sorrows of the people. They expect to meet people who prefer that PVs didn't come to their nation, making them appreciate so much more the far greater numbers who recognize efforts and make a point to show their appreciation.

Knowing this, remarks of the young men after President Kennedy's death didn't permanently dismay me for around the corner were better days. I'll not forget the Aymara Indian mother who came from her wretched hut behind a wall and was standing outside the Balconcillo church after the Memorial Mass for President Kennedy. Catching the attention of several Yankees, we could hear as she sobbed out her sorrow to us:

"He sent milk for my baby."

CHAPTER XI

GROWTH OF THE POPE'S VOLUNTEERS

"The test of our progress is not whether we add
more to the abundance of those who have
much; it is whether we provide enough for
those who have too little."
— Franklin Delano Roosevelt

Slowly, inevitably, the life of the beloved Pope John, whose reign
was to last less than five years, was drawing to a close. This outstanding but humble man, the Papal Volunteers' first "boss," had
lost much sleep because of the pitiful condition of the Church in
Latin America. One who knows personally of the former pontiff's
gnawing, tortured feelings is the Maryknoller, Father John J. Considine, director of the Latin American Bureau for the United States
Catholic Conference in Washington, D. C.

"The need to strengthen the Church in Latin America was an
intense concern of His Holiness, Pope John XXIII, a concern mani-
fested in one of the first acts of his pontificate, and in one of his last,"
Father Considine said.

In 1960 Pope John summoned religious and lay leaders of the
Catholic world and told them "the Latin American Church could
not be limited to the very notable efforts put forth up to the present.
Personnel must be found and sent there in the greatest numbers
possible."

Three years later when Pope John died, the great worldwide sadness was felt doubly by Papal Volunteers who had answered his call to the foreign missions. That Mary Ellen and I actually were in a Latin American land, doing what we could to extend the wishes of Pope John, is an experience that we shall always regard as an honor and privilege.

Columns of our little, unofficial PAVLA newspaper from Peru, *La Idea,* in its June, 1963, issue, joined in the expression of universal mourning at the death of Pope John. One of the purposes of *La Idea* was to reflect the good will of the people who supported PAVLA's early efforts. PVs wondered where money would come from to pay bills of *La Idea* after we met in January of 1963 and all enthusiastically approved such a publication to inform people at home of our activities in the field. The printer said that 500 copies of the initial issue would cost about $20. "Oh, but you want it printed in English? Then double as much," he added as he plucked another piece of type out of the case with ink-stained hands and clicked it into place in his compositor's stick. We began plans to get the project going, collecting copy and photos, sending letters to would be benefactors, deciding to place no price on the paper in order to avoid involvement with Peruvian tax laws.

On the last day of February we launched our non-profit venture. A letter from Rev. William C. O'Connor, C.S.C., pastor of the parish, St. Francis Xavier, in Burbank, Calif., contained a check for $49, nine dollars more than needed for the initial printing. *La Idea* was on the way.

"A couple in the parish," Father Bill wrote, "had a stroke of luck recently. I suspect it was either at Las Vegas or Santa Anita. They didn't say so I didn't ask questions. The other night the husband handed me $49 with instructions to send it to a friend in the mission fields. It gives me real delight to be able to pass this along to you."

Upon receipt of his first copy, an ambassador of Pope John, Archbishop Romolo Carboni, Apostolic Nuncio to Peru, encouragingly wrote: "May I take this opportunity to congratulate you for your generous contribution to the Papal Volunteer movement in Peru."

From Cardinal Juan Landazuri Ricketts, Primate of Peru, came the message:

"We are sure that *La Idea* will bring to many sectors of the United States a captivating story of the possibilities for action in these parts for new volunteers, creating together with a tremendous effort of Christian charity and apostolate, a stronger and more intimate relation between both peoples, destined to produce a beneficial reward for all."

The Papal Volunteers' newspaper, which grew to one bumper Christmas issue of 2,100 copies, was a collective effort to effect a smoother-running organization in Peru and provide PV information for people in the U. S. who cared about their spiritual and material needs after they arrived.

For the first year or so that the PAVLAns were on the Peruvian scene, from mid-1961 on, there was a buckling-down to the newness as the first half dozen PVs got into the swing of teaching, nursing, and youth work. The trail-blazers were encouraged as they looked around one day, discovered that their numbers had increased to a dozen in Peru. Some six months later the total had increased to 24 PVs on duty in Peru, scattered throughout the coastal and altiplano parishes. In another year Papal Volunteers, numbering about 35 men and women in Peru alone, had increased two and three times faster than newly-arriving religious communities from the states who involved themselves in the ten percent personnel plan suggested by Pope John. We wondered as annual retreat time approached where we could find facilities for our growing numbers. The IHM sisters generously offered a school room and spacious private patio for Sunday days of recollection each month, but three days' board and room for 25 or 30 PVs was something different. On free days, PVs were bothered by the universal problem of boredom. What could we do? Where could we go to get a little change of pace? Entertainment funds didn't figure much in PV budgets. Already we were aware of center-houses that some longer-established religious groups had, where priests, nuns, and brothers could find relaxation. Besides there was a pressing need for at least a PV office in Lima, a corner with a desk, file cabinet, and typewriter where necessary PV paper work of Peruvian identity cards, travel papers, and the like could be processed. For the first handful of PAVLA arrivals Father James Connell, a Maryknoll veteran in Peru with unbending allegiance to his native San Francisco, punched out a ream of official papers, selflessly helping PAVLA past exasperating red tape, helping the new group to get on its feet. Often, when he'd punish the typewriter, filling out forms in Spanish, I'd think about the Maryknoll booklet reviewing the Golden Anniversary of the order (1911–1961). On one of the pages affable Father Connell was pictured at a typewriter high in the Andes mountains at a parish post near Lake Titicaca. An altiplano Indian wearing his warm, striped, home-spun pancho and with a colorful chullo cap pulled down over his ears was saying: "My name is Juan Quispe, Padre," and Father Connell's fingers, chilled from the high sierra air, thumped the keyboard filling in a church or government form for the un-schooled Indian. Nearby on the wall was a crank-type telephone, a calendar of moveable feast days, and a Crucifix. After we started ganging up on him for administrative help, we often thought that it would be easier for him to be back among the guys wearing the panchos and knit caps. If he himself ever thought it — God bless him for all the good he did for the Papal Volunteers — he never let on. Still it didn't take much reflection to decide it was about time that our PAVLA team in Peru, growing steadily as it was, had its own office and manager.

From high sierra assignments PVs would arrive in Lima for the month's required rest leave out of every six to balance up the red and white corpuscle count, and it was a sad state of affairs because they had no place to stay. Certainly the time was overdue for a PAVLA centerhouse in Lima. It was all fine, good, and charitable to double and triple up in our apartments, making room for the visitors from the hills, the PVs just in from Latin American training centers, PVs in transit or in ailing health. But the Lima PVs with daily work schedules to maintain and PVs on vacation with their irregular hours agreed that a month of such poles-apart scheduling was not the best. Some PVs didn't relish coming out of the hills for required rest leave only to be forced into crowded living conditions in Lima. On PV money it wasn't possible to pay prices of pensións or hotels. Watch-ing this problem develop, we started discussing a PAVLA regional centerhouse that would adequately accommodate PVs from Ecuador,

Peru, Bolivia, and Chile. But the first need was for an office with permanent clerical help.

The Lima Regional Center finally established in March of 1964 was one of the bonuses of our PAVLA assignment. Chicago headquarters, sending David O'Shea, national secretary then, on a Latin swing of PAVLA posts, turned on the green light and centerhouse planning began. As the PVs began arriving at the new location from the mountains for rest and recreation leave, their obvious appreciation and happiness completely justified every effort expended on obtaining the center.

"Heartfelt congratulations on the historic occasion of the blessing of the centerhouse" was the message received in the center's office of PV Field Representative Kevin Dwyer from Rev. Raymond Kevane, national director in Chicago. Much credit for the initial backing of the center goes to Father Considine, who when contacted by amateur radio hookup from Lima to Washington, D. C., okayed planning set up by Dwyer with Father Victor R. Fernandez, S.J., first National Director for PAVLA. Approval and financial support of the Pontifical Commission for Latin America in Rome followed and the new center was rented for its first two years of operations, a lease since extended. Historic PAVLA days were recorded at the new center in August of 1964 due to the visits of Cardinal Landazuri on the 18th and of Cardinal Cushing on the 19th. The visit of Cardinal Landazuri included its official formal blessing and opening. Cardinal Cushing took time from the crowded visitation schedule of his foundation, the Pious Society of St. James the Apostle, and, arriving early on the morning of August 19 after an exhausting trip to Bolivia, said the first Mass for PVs in their home away from home. Twenty-two of the seventy PVs then assigned to the four-nation area of Ecuador, Peru, Bolivia, and Chile were at the center, serving as delighted hosts during those momentous events.

PAVLA, indeed, had arrived on the west coast of South America after those significant events. J. Wesley Jones, U. S. ambassador to Peru, was among the 110 guests attending the house blessing. Our ambassador was aware of PV work, having met some volunteers in his Peruvian travels and through his wife and daughters.

Papal Volunteers' days of knocking on the doors of U. S. religious communities for assistance — followed by several groups' splendid cooperation — ended with the new hustle and activity in the Regional Center, where PVs could in return invite religious over for social gatherings. A milestone was passed. For some heady days after the departure of the two Cardinals, PVs had their moments in the sun, asking priests who'd stop by for a visit or on business if they had an appointment, or would they please wait until after the bishop has left, or informing them that "we'll have a half hour free before His Excellency arrives."

When leaving their home diocese for training schools or mission posts, Papal Volunteers invariably visit with their bishop for an appropriate departure ceremony which includes a Mass, during which they receive their mission cross from the hands of their Ordinary. Mary Ellen and I received these from affable Archbishop Edward J. Hunkeler in Kansas City, Kansas. Since Mary Ellen was raised in the Wichita diocese and completed nursing training there, Kansas PV directors asked if, as the first married couple, we would leave from that diocese in the hope of creating interest perhaps among other couples. So, at St. Mary's Cathedral in Wichita, Bishop Mark K. Carroll also presented us copies of the New Testament and crosses as we joined two other PVs, Virginia Messerschmidt and Mary Griffing, in departure ceremonies.

Our launching into mission orbit from Wichita — although we did not realize it at the time — occurred at the "Bethlehem" of PAVLA. Father Michael J. Lies, who for almost five years served as national assistant director of PAVLA, said that on January 27, 1961, Bishop Carroll published a statement introducing the diocesan PAVLA program as the first in the United States. His Excellency remarked:

"Pope John XXIII has called attention to the urgent need of the Church in Latin America and sends out a plea to the world, especially to the United States and Canada, to come to its aid. The Holy Father asks for lay volunteers to give their talent, time, and treasures; to stand beside the Latin Americans to help form and strengthen their Church. To the generous people who cooperate with his plan, the Holy Father gives the honorary title of 'Papal Volunteers.'"

At the 21st annual Jesuit Mission dinner at the Waldorf Astoria in New York on November 7, 1963, after we had completed our first two years in Peru, Father Lies was to receive well-earned honors and the Xavier Award for "outstanding zeal and dedication to the missions." There he joined the ranks of such other mission honorees as Cardinals Samuel Stritch, Francis Spellman, and Richard Cushing, and the Maryknoll bishop, The Most Rev. James E. Walsh, a prisoner of the Chinese Reds. Such recognition helped buoy us along the way, as also did the letters from Archbishop Carboni, who took time from the business of the Vatican Council to write us:

"It was my great privilege to have a private audience with His Holiness, Pope Paul VI (Oct. 5, 1964). Once again I was struck by the intimate knowledge which the Holy Father evidences in the affairs of Peru. I spoke of your work and the Pope smiled with great satisfaction. Please be assured that you do not work alone. The Pope knows of you, he loves you, he is most grateful for the dedicated and fruitful work you are rendering to the Church in Peru, and lovingly he blessed you and your work."

And another time he wrote:

"You are always in my thoughts in a special way when I am in Rome, for you are Papal Volunteers, but this time I thought of you more than ever because of all the attention which the Conciliar Fathers gave to the apostolate of the layman.

"You would have been proud and thrilled as I was myself, to have heard two laymen address the Council in formal session, one of whom, your compatriot, spoke in Latin! Mr. Patrick Keegan of England spoke movingly and very effectively of the role of the layman in the Church's apostolic life and pleaded for more qualified priests to work with the lay movements. He was warmly applauded.

"Mr. James Norris, of the Catholic Relief Services in New York, made a splendid impression on the assembled Fathers when he spoke of the problem of hunger in the world. I think that many Bishops made a resolve to tap the rich mine of lay apostles in their dioceses, after hearing Mr. Norris."

Usually twice annually we were invited to the residence of Archbishop Carboni for a progress conference, discussion of problems, and a bountiful dinner. To visit with His Excellency following his return from Vatican Council II sessions spiritually re-enforced our service in Peru.

The diversity of the PAVLA work, personal contacts, and mail received — sometimes from complete strangers — were other rewarding experiences as the program grew.

Two weeks after the Apostolic Nuncio's warm message in 1964 a letter arrived from a Californian we had (and have) never met. She wrote offering financial assistance to the Tapia family. This housewife, herself a Latin American who had moved from Bogotá, Colombia, had a beautiful message, expressed in her new acquired English:

"I have before me the Maryknoll magazine from this month and in one of the pages you write story of this lovely family, Mrs. Tapia and her nine children. I wish to send her at least $10 every month poor soul I know how sad this life is. In the name of the Infant Jesus I am doing this, He left us to help one another. Is so much need.

"My angel mother used to work for thirty cents a day washing and ironing clothes, many times we went to bed without food. My precious father was very poor, too, and I couldn't see it right to see so much hunger, I went to beg many times for my people. I know what it is to be hungry and the worst thing, I never found anyone who can reach the hand for a piece of bread.

"I want to reach this lady," she concluded, not before mentioning that she, too, had gone to work in an office like the eldest of the Tapia girls. "I can't describe in words temptations and abuses that I received from men and I will pray for this little girl that may God keep this child innocent as they are, is no better life."

Pains as well as joys are part of any developing program and PAVLA reveled in the former just as certainly as it could not escape the latter. About a dozen of us Kansas program people comprised the thirty or so volunteers working Peruvian territory in those early days. Occasionally, we managed to meet in Lima for a bull session about our work, about the good old days, and about plans for coming months. Gripes were heard here and there and invariably we Kansans would have to defend the hotly-discussed *Guidebook for Latin American Missioners,* which was written by Kansas directors when PAVLA was just in its beginnings and when someone had to construct the complex for the launching of the first rocket. The guidebook was that initial exploratory rocket so to speak; and it took some real buffeting from PVs, but it stayed on course, its mission shaky at times but never scrubbed.

Some of the guidebook's suggestions were touched upon lightly in previous chapters of this book covering spiritual formation. Daily Mass, frequenting of the sacraments, daily spiritual reading, rosary, nightly examen, daily visits to the Blessed Sacrament. All of these certainly are basic to the success of any sort of Catholic apostolic endeavor. Yet, the book which was later suggested for national, not just Kansas, use, infuriated some volunteers.

"We're mature people!"

"We don't need such a primer!"

The Kansans weren't hinting that anyone should follow the book's line. However, after changing some initial regulations, volunteers put the guidebook to the field test and learned that the rule, for example, that slacks were not to be worn by girls in public, was simply unworkable when the girls in youth recreation programs put it to the test. The guidebook authors thought Peruvian girls or Latin American girls didn't wear slacks in public. The fact was, however, that stretch pants and slacks in public were so popular among the rising middle class — and wealthy, as to give the impression that these articles of apparel had been invented below the border!

Dating is prohibited, the guidebook said. But the single girls learned that an escort was needed after dark, so there was some necessary dating among PVs for reasons of safe travel to a movie or a night out to relax. In the main, PV girls went out in small groups anyway, or would team up to use some pastor's car for a night of relaxation. Veteran religious superiors of PVs, cognizant of the machismo outlook, were guided accordingly in controlling dating regulations between the North Americans and the South Americans. Several times happy marriages of PVs and Latin Americans took place after their three-year terms ended. Some quit the program to get married before terms were completed.

"Write sponsors weekly," the guidebook said. At first this was workable until assignments multiplied and demanded more and more of the PVs' time. However, letters from sponsors fell off appreciably also, and one PV went two and a half years before her first personal letter arrived from the group sponsoring her. Sponsors should not feel, nor should program directors feel, that the regular monthly allotment from sponsor to director is their "letter" to the field volunteer. People received hearts before pocketbooks, a fact that can't be overlooked in Papal Volunteer or any other work.

When lay people volunteer for apostolic work in distant lands, it is expected that screening, or their own personal maturity, will help determine that they are grown enough to understand, for example, why career missioners among priests, brothers, and nuns have regular spiritual re-enforcement along the mission trails. Of course, a rebel or two gets to Latin America, or one too immature, and it was eye-opening to watch how such a one's words could confuse some in the group. In the main, there was little muted whining.

If PVs are going to do, or attempt, mission work, there should be no quarrel about maintaining necessary spiritual formation while in the field. A parable might be told here: A few years ago, after the value of the boliviano currency skidded to a point where thousands of household necessities, a man in La Paz was pushing a wheelbarrow piled high with Bolivian folding money on his way to the grocery store for a few staples. Two armed holdup men jumped from behind a fence, dumped the huge pile of bolivianos on the sidewalk and made off with the wheelbarrow!

One might see the values of PAVLA in the wheelbarrow in contrast to that of the nation's money. Success of PAVLA work requires, as any other venture, that the whole of the program be considered. Somebody has to have a firm grip on the wheelbarrow or many, many good intentions come to nothing.

For instance, among PAVLA people there was a debate whether only top skilled, seasoned, well-educated people should be sent. Is it better to send only a few highly qualified volunteers, or to send many even if among those many not all are polished experts in their fields or able to master the foreign language? Some lay groups direct their people to learn as they go in the nation to which they have been assigned: To learn the language while mixing with the people; about the widespread ignorance of their Church on the part of Latin Americans; about extending Christian charity below the border by example. Others, notably PAVLA's latest training programs here in the U. S. and below the border, accept as fact a need for advance training.

PAVLA and other lay directors in the U. S. must toss in their sleep over candidate selection. Will the Phi Beta Kappa-type fall flat on his face under the Latin American customs and culture? Will the former truck driver turned Papal Volunteer win many people to his heart and to the Church, doing more for the latter's eternal gain despite the fact that he has great difficulty with the Spanish or Portuguese language? How many priests in Latin America wouldn't like to have the unsophisticated, nonchalant Papal Volunteer who can teach catechism or build a convent and who in his unassuming manner writes it off by saying "Anyone who can use his head and his hands can be used down here"? What about the diocesan director who has turned back a half dozen prospects because they failed the psychiatric tests? "Yet," the director told us, "three of them had excellent talents and the loss seemed very great. We were tempted to chuck the psychiatric reports. So far we haven't." On the other hand, there was the director of a lay volunteer group who said that they don't put too much emphasis on those reports. What about the youth worker whom the kids followed around the parish like the Pied Piper — the one who admitted that his high school diploma represented a real struggle?

After being there, after seeing the action, we don't concur entirely with the idea of sending only the few holding very high IQs. Occasionally, as we have seen, this is the "volunteer" who passes up the work, not recognizing it or not wanting to, so that it goes undone until the high school graduate of lower intelligence appears and does it. Certainly the hard and ordinary tasks are often passed by the "schooled" Latin who knows that some of the "peons" will do it. It was strange (to us), on one parish outing with families along the seashore, to observe that the Papal Volunteers, both men and women, did the bulk of the work in getting the tents up, the campsite in order, and later, did most of the work of breaking camp, such as folding the tents, and carrying them to the truck. Most of the Latins just sat talking, until we felt it was time they helped. When we asked them to help, they did. But the philosophy "We don't do things that way here" has shown signs of slowly changing.

Good will alone is not enough either for the lay volunteer. Something sound must accompany the spark of goodness — be it the talent for laying bricks, nursing, teaching, or whatever. And, as some training schools send people even with little language proficiency, these people will have some obvious talent, along with apostolic zeal, to get a job done if they are indeed sincere. It is an interesting fact that Maryknollers, in voting on the fellow priests who did the most inspiring and beneficial work in a couple of west coast nations of South America, selected three men who had the toughest battle with the language.

One week on C.I.C. assignment I photographed a couple of onions, two eggs, some cheese, chopped peppers, and a tomato. These items were next to a two-burner kerosene stove upon which two pots of water were bubbling to a boil. All of this action took place under a lean-to enclosure in a close-quartered corralon slum in Lima's La Victoria district. This sounds like a flat sort of "scoop" assignment; but the picture story centered around a young Peruvian social worker demonstrating to about fifty mothers the knack of getting more nutrition from using these foods mixed with the trigor wheat flour, powdered milk, and other staples distributed through Peru's Caritas program in collaboration with Catholic Relief Services and the U. S. government.

When the water was boiling, the ingredients were put into it. When cooked, the result was a thick, tasty soup which the social worker invited the women to sample, telling them all the while how the better taste also meant stronger bodies. Mothers got the idea; why cook one or two Caritas foods separately, and less tastefully, when the combined package has so much more appeal? What was amazing to me was how few words the Peruvian social worker spoke while she chopped peppers, cracked eggs, then pitched everything into the pots. A PAVLA social worker could have done the same thing even if her language had not yet become fluent. Very few of those slum mothers had ever held a textbook in their hands anyway, and they were certainly bending the language rules in their Spanish-Quechuan mixture. Volunteers of good will and talent could ferret out those Latins with social welfare abilities. Many women in Latin America can make soup. More of them must be found, with the desire to help their countrymen rise from the miseries of an underprivileged existence.

Again, apropos of language needs, one evening Mary Ellen and I were walking toward the Regional Center when from out of the darkness we heard a child's scream followed by continued wailing not only from the child but from a woman who was mumbling excitedly in her guttural, Indian tones. As they emerged from the shadows, we saw them — three children clustered close to their mother's bulky skirt, and a baby in a sling around her back. Avenida Arequipa, where the street lamp lighted the scene, was alive with rushing traffic. We approached the corner, paused, and greeted the mother as Mary Ellen crouched down to say "Hola, niño!" to a crying boy with a viciously deep laceration across the inside of his index finger on the right hand. The blood flowing over the rest of his hand made it look even worse. With a tissue from her handbag, Mary Ellen daubed the wound, applying pressure to stop the flow of blood. Making a bandage from a handkerchief, she wrapped the cloth around the finger and tied it firmly. The tears stopped. Hearing her "Muchas gracias, Señora" convinced us of the woman's gratitude. Motioning in the direction of the hospital, we told the mother to stop there for more treatment and she said "Sí, sí, sí"; whether she did it, or understood or not, is another thing. But for the moment at least there had been some help for her. We all walked to the center boulevard strip, where we waited for a letup in the traffic so that the family could get to the other side — where they disappeared into the darkness.

For the unschooled campesinos time, distances, and the future are quite beyond their comprehension; their measurements of things are not ours. The mother was sure she'd reach the hospital with her son who needed treatment, if not in the ten-minute walk which it was, then maybe tomorrow or the day after, and if she needed another bandage for the finger in the meantime she'd wrap a leaf around it. These people trudge incredible distances to market, church, or to reach Lima and Utopia. Or one of them will sit on a boulder in the sierra for the longest time without moving, waiting for a new idea maybe, waiting for someone to come along and ask him to dig potatoes or watch the sheep.

One padre asked his penitent how long since his last confession and the man replied quickly: "Un ratito, padre." For the Latins this means, or compares normally to, "a little while" as we know it. The priest wanted to be exact. A week? No. Month? No. Six months, a year? No. "How long?" the priest asked. "Three years," came the reply.

To people living in the hills for generations there is small need for exactness. The penitent carried no calendar in his hip pocket wallet. Most likely he had no wallet. There was no calendar on his choza hut wall; if in luck, he might find one on the bulletin board outside the mayor's office. He hears distant church bells in the village. Is it Sunday or a feast of the village's patron saint? He might not get there for either. If Pedro does get there to join his countrymen, it's the happy priest who can complete his spiritual schedule with the Indians before fiesta revelry and merriment erupt because who is to say when their fun will cease?

When we visited with Monsignor Robert Walton, busy at Coripata's St. James church in the Bolivian hills, a July week of merriment in observance of the nation's Independence Days was well under way. Campesinos' gaiety in the streets, well into the third day, meant a cut back, of course, for the normal church schedule. Cancelled, too, that night, was the movie normally following services. As we conducted our business in the parish, we saw more of the Latin culture unfold . . . street dances on cobblestones, seven individual bands, seven different tunes from seven locations along the blocks, and then there was time out for an assault on the case of beer which the musicians carried with them in their wandering. In remote, pretty little mountain villages it's understandable why customs are at odds with ideal, daily patterns of a spiritual life. In the large cities, however, if Lima is any sample, there are ample opportunities for people to remain informed on Church matters. The newspapers carry announcements such as the following:

"To Catholics: Tomorrow, Wednesday, 7th, *La Prensa* will publish a list appearing in alphabetical order relating to the Churches of Lima, Callao and districts, and some neighboring areas, indicating hours and days in which they will have Lenten Masses, baptism and confessions."

Happily, the Lenten season does bring many more people into the churches.

Our Papal Volunteer regional center was without a chapel for its first several months of operation and most concerned over this lack was Mary Ellen who, as administrator of the center's room and board program, quietly began a chapel campaign. Her project reached fruition ultimately when Father Denis McAuliffe, a Chicago province Domini-can — who had assisted the Kansas PAVLA program's formation of early candidates while a college instructor in Salina — said the first Mass in the small chapel on the first Sunday of December, 1964. Father McAuliffe, who left his Kansas assignments when named to the Dominicans' missions in Bolivia, brought valued and interesting dia-logue to the center while he took weekends off from the language and culture training center. He could have been listed as the first unofficial chaplain for the PVs in their center. Both Father Garrity and a St. James the Apostle Society priest, Father Joseph Martin, had celebrated Masses earlier in the center but those were in beginning days when each Mass meant special permission from the archbishop's office un-til the center's permanent altar was constructed and the chapel opened. Mary Ellen's appeal to religious communities working in Lima brought vestments, altar linens, chalices, missals, and other needs as nine groups responded generously. Cash from Queen of the Holy Rosary church in Overland Park, Kansas, covered much of the cost for the construction of the altar.

Permission for the Blessed Sacrament to be reserved in the perma-nent tabernacle of the chapel where daily, or at least weekly, Mass could be said, was obtained at the chancery. Next the chalice would have to be consecrated. My wife and I selected one of three donated to the chapel, took a taxi to Plaza de Armas in downtown Lima, and entered a small chapel just to the left of the grand cathedral.

Monseñor Fidel Tubino, auxiliary bishop of Lima in charge while Cardinal Landazuri was away attending the third session of Vatican

Council II, came out of the sacristy, his red socks flashing when he genuflected in front of the tabernacle. He motioned for us to come up into the sanctuary, where we stood off to the gospel side while he consecrated the chalice.

"Should a donation be left for the chapel," we asked Monseñor Tubino.

"This is for the Voluntarios del Papa," he replied. "It's our part of help in your work for us. Please say a Hail Mary for me before leaving the chapel." We shook hands and kissed the episcopal ring.

The taxi returning us to the center had left Detroit's assembly line at least eighteen years before, so it transported us slowly toward Lince with our precious cargo in the shoe box between us on the back seat. It had a loose bearing and the motor sounded as if a piston rod would tear a hole into the side of the engine block at any moment but didn't.

A month earlier I had met a North American priest at the Hotel Bolivar for a trip to the slum-ridden Comas district.

"Taxi?" shouted the driver coming across the sidewalk toward us, a couple paces ahead in the rush of drivers seeking fares.

And he led us off toward the curb where from among a string of shiny, unmarked private vehicles awaiting business from the hotel trade he opened the door of a still-new limousine, sparkling like it was just a couple days old. "Momentito, señor," I said to the driver, holding back the visiting clergyman from entering. Our mission was to the slums. How could the taxi driver have known that we, approaching from the grand entrance of the Bolivar, were not on our way to a country club, the race track, or one of the embassies? We thanked him kindly, telling him our destination. It wasn't necessary to explain further. He wouldn't want his elegant motor car bouncing around Comas' rocky, unpaved streets, maybe inviting a stray stone thrown from around the corner of a straw shanty, or a pail of slop timed to splash the shiny paint job. Our point was clear. Around the corner, down La Colmena a half block, where you can flag down assorted taxis from today's brand to something going back to the first Roosevelt administration, we hailed a cab recognized as a new model when President Eisenhower was in his first year on Capitol Hill.

Nearing Lince with the Regional Center chapel treasures, I thought to myself that a shiny, ultra-fine car would have been more appropriate for the objects we carried — vessels that would soon hold the Body and Blood of Christ. Then I remembered that the very first chapter of His whole wonderful record began simply indeed, in a stable, and I wondered if perhaps He may not prefer simple things.

CHAPTER XII

WHERE PINEAPPLE IS SWEETEST

"I turned myself to other things: and I saw the
oppressions that are done under the sun, and the
tears of the innocent. And they had no com-
forter. And they were not able to resist their
violence, being destitute of help from any."
— Ecclesiastes, Ch. 4

As often as we'd been there to welcome PVs from training schools
in Mexico or Puerto Rico, to greet touring clergymen and laity on the
Peruvian leg of their continental travels, or to bid adieu to departing
PAVLA veterans, one special day arrived when, homeward bound
ourselves, we approached Lima's Jorge Chavez International Airport.
Happily enough, but as if all too suddenly, it was three years since
we first crossed into Latin American territory on the bus at Laredo.
Five hours late but sweeping in from the south as though it was setting a new record for being on time, the plane arrived from Chile.
Amid the flurry of passenger activity, servicing the plane, jubilant
greetings and touching farewells there was heard over the public address the call for passengers — first in Spanish, then repeated in English — and we boarded. From our windows as the plane lifted off the
runway, we could see dots of people on the observation deck — and
thought how often we had been among all of those dots. Below them
was a neat row of larger dots — crated refrigerators from the U. S.
air freighted for speed and quicker profits, awaiting weeks or months
of import red tape to be untangled.

Straining toward space above adobe shacks in scattered slums fringing the airport, the jet giant in seconds pushed into the solid, silvery, coastal overcast. We had had our last look at Peru. Now, surrounded by the puffy white outside, we struggled with those departure thoughts we'd wondered about at times while on the job and not really concerned about them. Those thoughts did not exclude assorted regrets about leaving the apostolic work in the Land of the Incas, but there were joyful memories, too, and later on both were to return to delight or sadden us. We knew now the tears of those innocents in misery without the barest of comforts in life, and we remembered those who are not destitute — the gay, singing, dancing Peruvians. Along our way how many thousands of the Latin American millions had we seen in their paupers' surroundings? Did we deny a Latin a helping hand? How should the PAVLA mission experiences be best shared back home? This we wondered about because of one returned volunteer's letter describing with what deep attachment he had spoken of the missions to one group, and how within moments the discussion had switched to the new auto laundromat going up in the shopping center! Wait and see, we thought, wait and see.

Streaking to the west, the plane banked gracefully, the pilot heading it out over the Pacific ocean blotted from sight by the cloud layer below. As the swift return began, ahead were Mexico City, Texas, Tampa, where the winter wheat of next year's Kansas harvest was soon to surround us and the Latins, but not their problems, would be miles away.

Not all airplane pilots have seen one. Those who have speak warmly about "The Flyer's Cross." Under unusual conditions when the cloud layer below is just right, when the sun is positioned just so at the side of the plane, and the blue canopy overhead is empty even of the thinnest cirrus clouds, pilots or passengers might see it. Somewhere between Lima and Mexico City in the five and a half hour flight I looked below our seemingly motionless silver craft in the jet stream and there to the east was the Flyer's Cross, as if gently resting upon the smooth, white cloudbank.

How symbolic and delightful . . . seeing that cross on the return from mission country!

The airplane's long fuselage and slim wings reflected a shadow as the cross below; the sun off in the western sky contributed the ring encircling the cross. For several moments I saw it, impossible to attempt a photograph because of the window angle. Then it was gone. Among air trip memories, the 21st day of December in 1964 was my day of the Flyer's Cross.

Losing altitude for the approach to Mexico City, we had a post card view again of Popocatepetl, the spectacular mountain of love, that brought back memories of our flight south. Our PAVLA circle was gradually completing itself — Kansas, the mountain, Peru, Popocatepetl again, and the return to wheatlands.

Leaving a civilization "tortured by want" as á Kempis once wrote, we were returning to our nation "weakened by pleasure." Hopefully, along our path ahead, those three years of lay mission commitment wouldn't be placed too far in the background though we'd be miles from needs of the underdeveloped areas. Many would be the occasions, said an Irish priest from Cork, to help explain those needs as seen in our little patch below the border, opportunities to promote the U. S. laity's new place in the Mystical Body.

Papal Volunteers ought to feel close to the late Pope John and his successor, but one day in Lima Mary Ellen learned just how distant we actually are from the chair of St. Peter. Wilfredo, a young Peruvian just hired as the Regional Center major-domo, was an alert type, possessing the vision needed to shape Peru's new future. Explaining the purpose of the PAVLA regional center, Mary Ellen outlined Willie's duties, told about the mission work, and pointed out that we were all volunteers for the Pope. Wide-eyed, Willie blurted out:

"Do you know the Pope?"

"Well, not exactly."

To Willie's Lima — the Mecca of Peru — we had bid farewell. She is Mecca because many citizens outside her feel that the nation's prestige, wealth, education, employment, and political power are concentrated there. "Tell me," a villager asked scornfully one day in the mountain community of Sicuani, "what do they care about us in Lima? They keep everything there!" Many of his friends, ripe for peaceful or violent revolution, think the same.

Decentralization — freeing people from the prison of Lima's slums and providing work for them in rich, but sparsely settled montaña country — is the driving goal of Belaunde. The montaña, east of the Andes mountains stretches to borders of Colombia, Brazil, Ecuador, and Bolivia, representing sixty-two percent of Peru's total land area, rich in timber, fruit, rubber, lumber, jute, and important grasslands for livestock grazing. Resources there remain untapped mainly because of limited overland access routes. Belaunde's dream, linked with Alliance for Progress money — a north-south highway east of the Andes — is under way to being fulfilled. It will bring in colonizers, take goods to market. "Adalante," shout current administration champions, "forward" to a new Peru. "No other government has ever really cared about the Indians or the common man," said one Lima economist of the current administration. "Belaunde has managed to awaken the campesinos — the millions who live in apathy and misery." With her economy growing stronger, Peru, once one of the poorest of Latin American nations, now has a per capita income of more than $250 annually, better, at least, than the $225 overall Latin average.

Passing from the economic phase to the spiritual, some opinions are more readily accepted when Cardinal Cushing, for example, expresses them as he did on the eve of one of his Latin American visits.

"One third of the world's baptized Catholics live in Latin America," the Cardinal said. "We could be losing them at a rate of a million a year. That is why I say our fight against communism centers in Peru, Bolivia, and Ecuador."

While in Peru we visited in dwellings of both extremes, the rich and the poor, and can strongly support Boston's archbishop in his observation:

"I'm appalled at the lack of social consciousness on the part of the fabulously wealthy. Why, some of them think they are wealthy by the will of God and that those poor masses are poor by the will of God."

At a time when illness weakened him, making his every effort a burden, Pope John commented in February of 1963:

"A remarkable number of religious, numbers of priests and laymen inflamed with the zeal for souls, have left their country spontaneously to go and work in the dioceses of Latin America.

"Their extraordinary eagerness and haste have already produced an abundant harvest of apostolic fruits. But joy arising from such examples of zeal and generosity is tempered by a vast concern each time we turn our attention toward the vast regions of Latin America where lives almost one third of the entire Catholic family.

"Although the dioceses of North America and Europe have already given precious and generous assistance, we realize fully that these people remain nevertheless crushed, overwhelmed by their multiple and urgent needs, and are in want of more basic help and on an even larger scale."

Mary Ellen and I were asked often why we were leaving for Latin America to work in the PAVLA program, and since our return have been asked why we went. Of our several reasons not the least is that Pope John called.

With our tour of Peruvian duty completed, we returned to the familiar midwestern countryside and were caught up again by the currents, the American way of life which adds up to man's search for happiness. From Lima's two million people, 500,000 of them in or near positive destitution, we returned to rural Tampa's 175 residents and the small town's change of pace.

In our frequent appearances before groups to talk PAVLA, and in our Midwest travels, people got away from asking about the poverty there — self-consciously in our land of plenty, they've heard enough about it; but the discussion has more than once turned to the high incidence of illegitimate births below the border. In astonishment about the whole set of social circumstances accounting for the hard fact, they mention an inch-deep newspaper filler placed just above the supermarket ad with the eye-catching headline:

ILLEGITIMATE BIRTHS

Datelined Lima, Peru, the filler unmistakably gained more readers' attention, buried as it was, than the item from the Indian Ocean island of Ceylon where a military group was reported as planning to overthrow the government, as the rumors went. Coup d'etats in the world are pretty common these days. Secretary of State Rusk reported

that 54 of them had occurred in a five-year period since President
Kennedy appointed him in 1961.

"Forty-three percent of Peru's births are illegitimate!" one reader
quoted in disbelief. We admitted that we knew that fact and
that some areas have as high as 48 percent and in some remote villages
the figures go unreported.

"But don't forget," we added, "those statistics reported from the
San Marcos university medical school in Lima did not cover their
slightly higher than fifty percent illiteracy. The report may have
had these figures originally, it may have been slashed by editors to
save space, but one ought not discuss Latin America's illigitimate
birth figures without considering, and with equal emphasis, the fact
of very high proportions of people without schooling."

Several weeks later the same newspaper carried another filler item
reporting that there are about 49 million domestic animals in Peru
and only 700 licensed veterinarians — one veterinarian for every
70,000 animals. Nobody ever brought up this astounding fact to us
in subsequent discussions.

Widespread illegitimacy is the prime Latin American problem, and
some of the social welfare PVs we exchanged views with gave an
assortment of reasons for it, not the least of which is lack of legisla-
tion to protect the mother. This reflects machismo's influence upon
men in position to ease the mother's plight. There are, besides the
cost of marriage, the shortage of priests — none in many remote areas,
and among unschooled people there is little notion of what the sacrament or civil ceremony are from the very outset. When a man finally
comes to the priest in Lima slums to have a marriage sacramentalized,
invariably he'll tell the priest something like "Padre, I haven't been
to church for over seven years." Then the priest has to determine if
it's his machismo showing or simply that there hadn't been a priest
for that many years and more in the village from which he migrated.

Peru has 52,000 centers of population comprised of only forty to
fifty families and less. Most of these settlements are scattered across
coast, mountain valleys, and jungles. Surprisingly, in most of them
there is a church of some kind, usually well maintained, ready for
use the moment a priest does arrive, unexpectedly or otherwise. More

and more, catechists are keeping religion alive and occasionally they are instrumental in bringing in a padre. How can authorities below the border reach all those isolated hamlet dwellers with medicines, education, employment, food, and religion . . . basics that are due them as human beings? Peru has only about a dozen cities of 25,000 or more inhabitants. In all but four we've worked on C.I.C. assignment or have visited on vacation, so we've experienced the dilemma of reaching the people out in the villages.

Back in our own land we've met several Peruvians, one of them Nancy Diaz, a 1966 graduate of St. Francis hospital school of nursing in Wichita. Only in the past decade has nursing in most Latin lands gained a public image placing it above domestic help, so we asked Nancy why she selected nursing. "I want to do something for our people who need help," was her reply and that moment was one of the most gratifying to us since returning to U. S. soil. Now, when people ask: "Do you really believe that PAVLA and all these aid programs will do any good down there?" we have only to begin talking enthusiastically about Nancy and the growing numbers of concerned Latins like her. When she visited us after graduation, she mentioned she was returning to work with her people near Tacna, a south Peru city where Father Fred Green, several Papal Volunteers, and other U. S. Jesuits work in the Cristo Rey parish and school. Father Green flew B-25s for the U. S. Marines in the South Pacific during World War II. Now his social justice efforts are most certainly hitting targets, shaking Peruvian aristocrats out of their oligarchical complacency. Father Green, like so many U. S. religious in the mission fields since World War II, exemplifies the new image of mission workers, people directly involved in building clinics, social welfare, and educational centers with the enthusiasm that early missionaries generated almost solely for chapel building and soul saving. Today, of course, it is recognized that the bodily needs have to be taken care of first, but this care cannot be separated from soul saving.

People who have approached us have quite regularly linked our work with that of the Peace Corps. "It's the same, isn't it?" The answer is that while we were involved with the social and economic urgencies of developing nations, our spiritual motives and contributions were never allowed to take secondary place in our considerations. Although PAVLA is openly promoted as God-centered and the Peace Corps is not, still some Peace Corps people evidence comparable motives. Free time for the Peace Corps volunteer, of course, is his own time and a handful of PCV Catholics and non-Catholics we met in Peru used some of that spare time to work directly with missionary priests and religious in Catholic centers. Our attraction to PAVLA simply reflects our preference for a Christian-centered, rather than a government-centered, program.

In the matter of volunteer effort we in this land should be aware that "Christian contributions" are being offered willingly by gradually increasing numbers of Latin American laity, people working oftentimes more effectively than gringo volunteers helping their downtrodden brothers in the Mystical Body. Some of these fine workers have left the comforts of upper or middle-class homes to teach in the jungles or the high sierras for periods ranging from the weeks or months of summer vacations to years of volunteer endeavor. A young woman of Lima's social set turned her back on days of sunbathing along the exclusive beaches of Ancon or dancing in the finer clubs of Lima and became involved instead in the Andean hills in arranging food allotments for hungry Indians, filling out forms to solemnize marriages, scheduling classes for the Peruvian catechists who could carry word of God's love to others. There are, indeed, many Latin American students who are not budding anarchists, ready to storm the palace or throw Molotov cocktails.

One of Lima's Papal Volunteer teachers and university scholarship liaison aides, Margaret Matesich, said: "In and out of San Marcos university I have become acquainted with the values and actions of many young Peruvians and have met some members of the Peruvian Peace Corps, the *Cooperación Popular Universitaria*. These students participate in a rigid formation program, training during evening free time and on Saturdays. Their summer vacation is spent working voluntarily on development projects in mountain and jungle Indian communities, experience which has served to make many of them interested in continued involvement in these critical areas of Peru after their university years are completed."

Since most university students in Latin America — outside the oligarchy — have to pay their own way, to sacrifice a summer vacation that could be spent on a paying job is a real contribution to the cause.

To just about every returning Papal Volunteer there comes at least one first invitation to talk and/or show slides explaining and illustrating his mission days. Contacted by program chairmen from various groups, we would consult the calendar and agree to another meeting and arrange to be away from home and to take off work. Some of the groups wanted only to be entertained for the evening or afternoon meeting; their interest in mission endeavor was secondary. To people who have given years to the missions the realization that such a meeting was seen only as a pitch to get the audience's money (a fact quite apparent at times) can tie a knot in the stomach. Our approach was this: "Our purpose here tonight is, hopefully, that we'll interest others in giving time and talent to urgent mission needs, giving these ideally in a Latin American mission post, or at least here at home helping through monetary assistance." Our appeal was the same whether our audiences were civic, Catholic, or Protestant church groups.

Are enough U. S. lay Catholics doing a fair share in carrying out our Christian duty to help mankind in less fortunate lands? Absolutely not. We're failing in this responsibility and know it. Our nation cannot any longer get by with the excuse that it is "too new" to send missionaries. U. S. maturity cannot be measured by Old World calendars because this nation has been favored with unheard of wealth; but we have not shown our appreciation in full measure, either spiritually or materially. We have the heart and the cash to be doing more than we are. On a per capita basis, U. S. Catholics are far behind other Christian denominations in mission support — both in manpower and finances.

No longer do my wife and I sit back in silence when we hear, "It's always the U. S. that's the goat for charity." During the Lenten season of 1959 West Germany's conference of Catholic bishops organized Misereor (meaning pity) which seeks as a group to rectify world distress by removing misery's causes rather than by battling the results of hunger, disease, illiteracy, and unemployment. The bishops proposed a continuing project to assist people regardless of color or creed. Betterment programs from Britain, France, and other nations too were seen in action in Peru. Young men and women, volunteer workers from nations other than the U. S., are on the scene and doing well in their projects. The U. S. is not "the goat for charity"! The U. S. is definitely not going it alone!

Is it difficult getting used to living in our own land again?

Do you think you'll ever go back to the missions?

These are other questions heard at PAVLA talks. Getting used to U. S. overabundance of material goods should be no chore, and it isn't. But for those who have lived amid hunger and handouts to return in less than eight hours to our bountiful tables and material plenty brings something of a shock.

One morning in tropical heat, as we stood just inside a monastery doorway out of the burning Peruvian sun, Brother Oscar asked us: "Would you like to accompany Father Arnoldo and me for tomorrow's Masses in our two mission chapels?" We eagerly accepted the invitation.

By the time the next day's last Mass had ended, we were hungry. The only cafe in the village was closed, but a villager sold us a large pineapple and with a sharp machete deftly whacked off its bristly sides, juice running along the blade with each stroke. Dividing it neatly into four sections, he picked up each part with the tip of the machete and handed one to each of us. Walking to the old car parked under a tree, we were silent as we ate the very delicious pineapple while listening to bird calls from deep within the jungle. One day we may find ourselves craving more of that superb pineapple. We might just have to have some. And you can't find its kind on our supermarket shelves.